DALSTON IN THE 80s

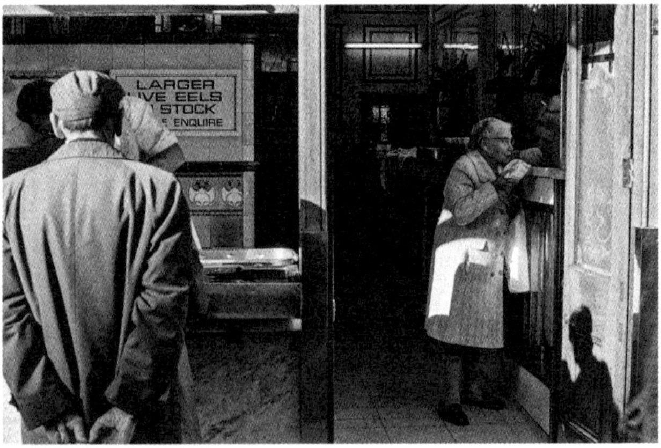
LARGER
EELS
STOCK
ENQUIRE

DALSTON IN THE 80s

by Andrew Holligan

HOXTON MINI PRESS

Other books in the series:

Book One
I've Lived in East London for 86½ Years

Book Two
East London Swimmers

Book Three
A Portrait of Hackney

Book Four
Shoreditch Wild Life

Book Five
One Day Young in Hackney

Book Six
Drivers in the 1980s

Book Seven
Columbia Road

Book Eight
Lost in the City

Book Nine
Hackney by Night

Book Ten
Sunday Football

Book Eleven
Along the Hackney Canal

Book Twelve
Adventures in the Lea Valley

Book Thirteen
Dalston in the 80s

East London Photo Stories

Book Thirteen

Dalston in the 80s
First Edition

All photographs © Andrew Holligan
Design and sequence by Friederike Huber, Andrew Holligan & Hoxton Mini Press
Series design by breadcollective.co.uk

A CIP catalogue record for this book is available from the British Library.

ISBN 978-1-910566-18-3

First published in the United Kingdom in 2017 by Hoxton Mini Press

Printed and bound by: 1010 Printing International Ltd.

To order books, collector's editions and signed prints please go to:
www.hoxtonminipress.com

MIX
Paper from responsible sources
FSC® C016973

"Our world, seemingly global, is in reality a planet of thousands of the most varied and never intersecting provinces. A trip around the world is a journey from backwater to backwater, each of which considers itself, in its isolation a shining star."

Ryszard Kapuściński

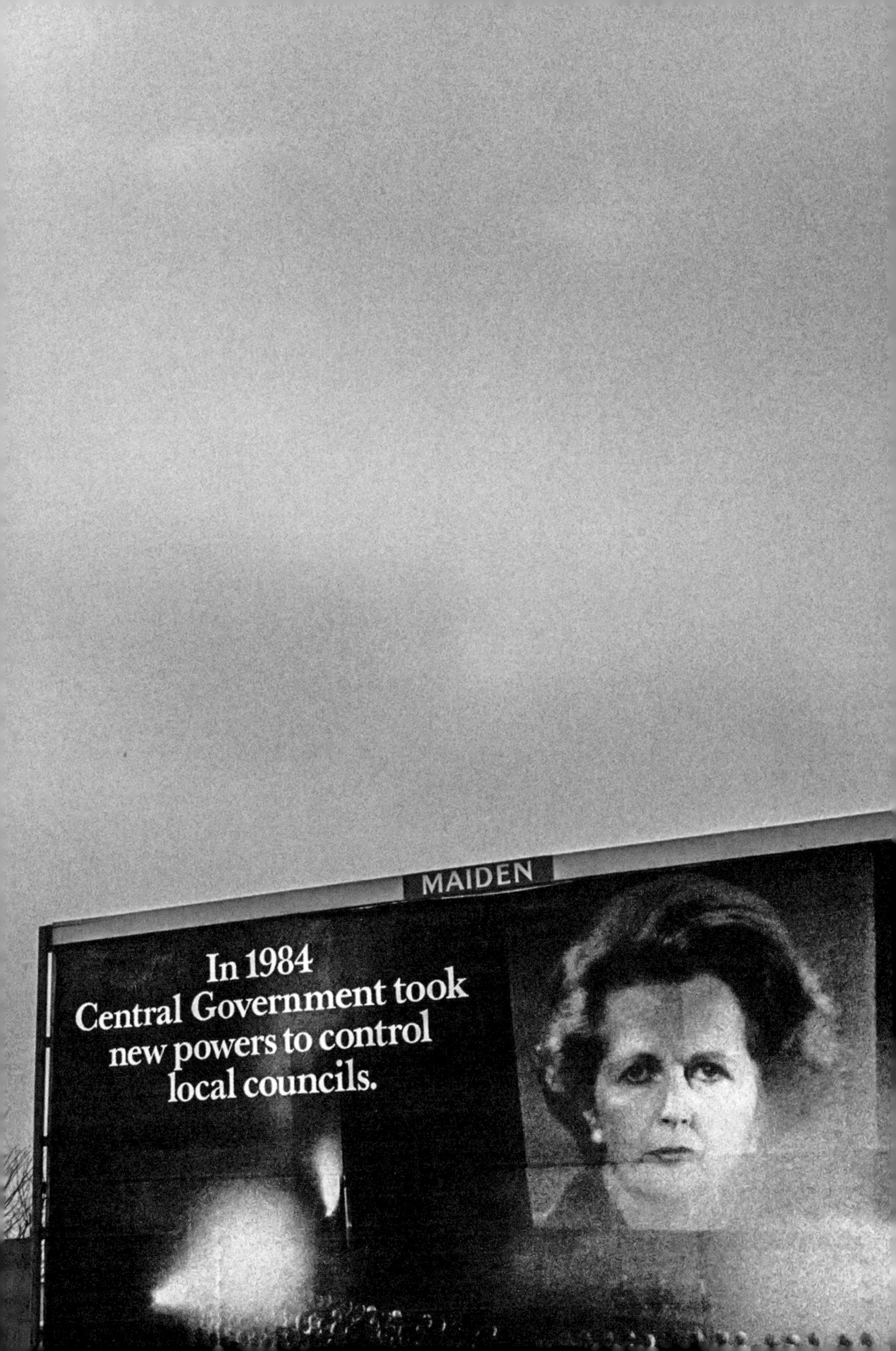
MAIDEN
In 1984
Central Government took
new powers to control
local councils.

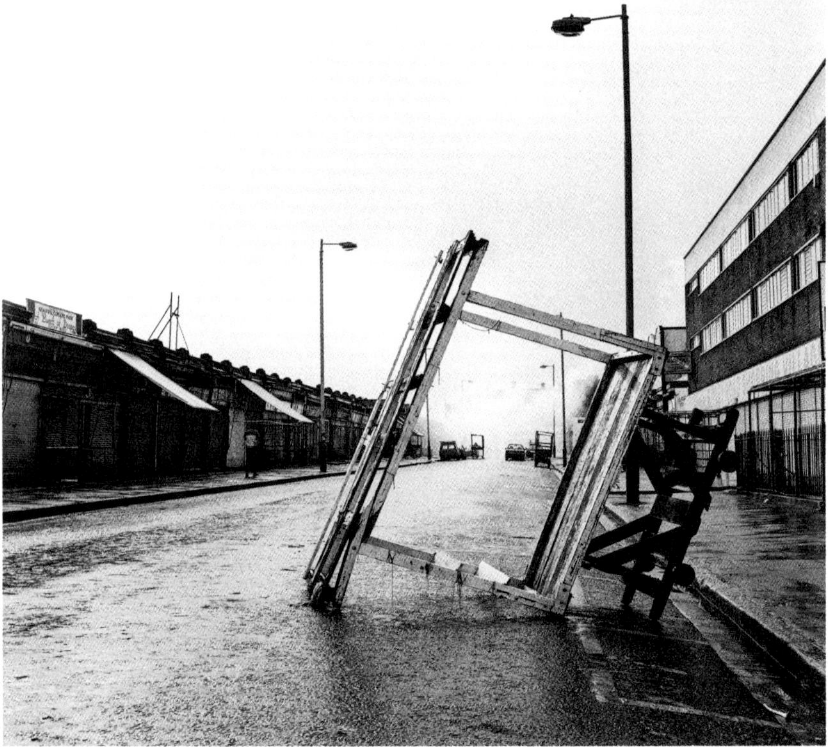

In the Spring of 1984
I moved to Dalston, East London.

I had been in New York City
working in the world of fashion photography
and it was time for a change.

After life in Manhattan,
Dalston felt like the back of beyond
and for my American wife it was:
"Not even a tube line!"

An old friend had offered me
his flat while he was "surfing"
in California.

It was a rambling place
above a bookmakers
just around the corner from
Ridley Road Market.

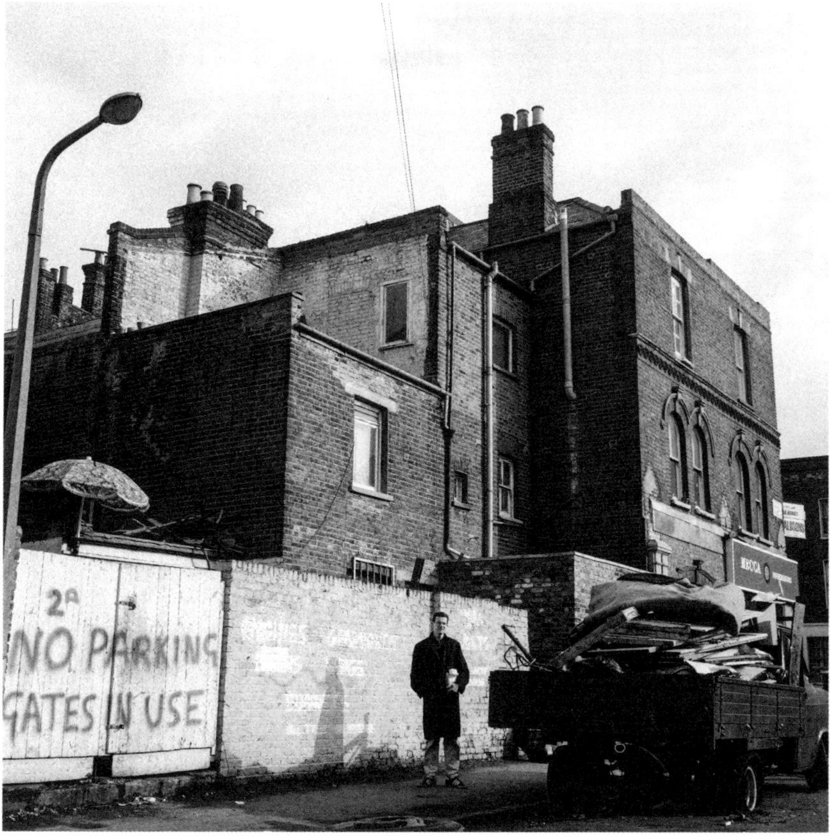
2a
NO PARKING
GATES IN USE

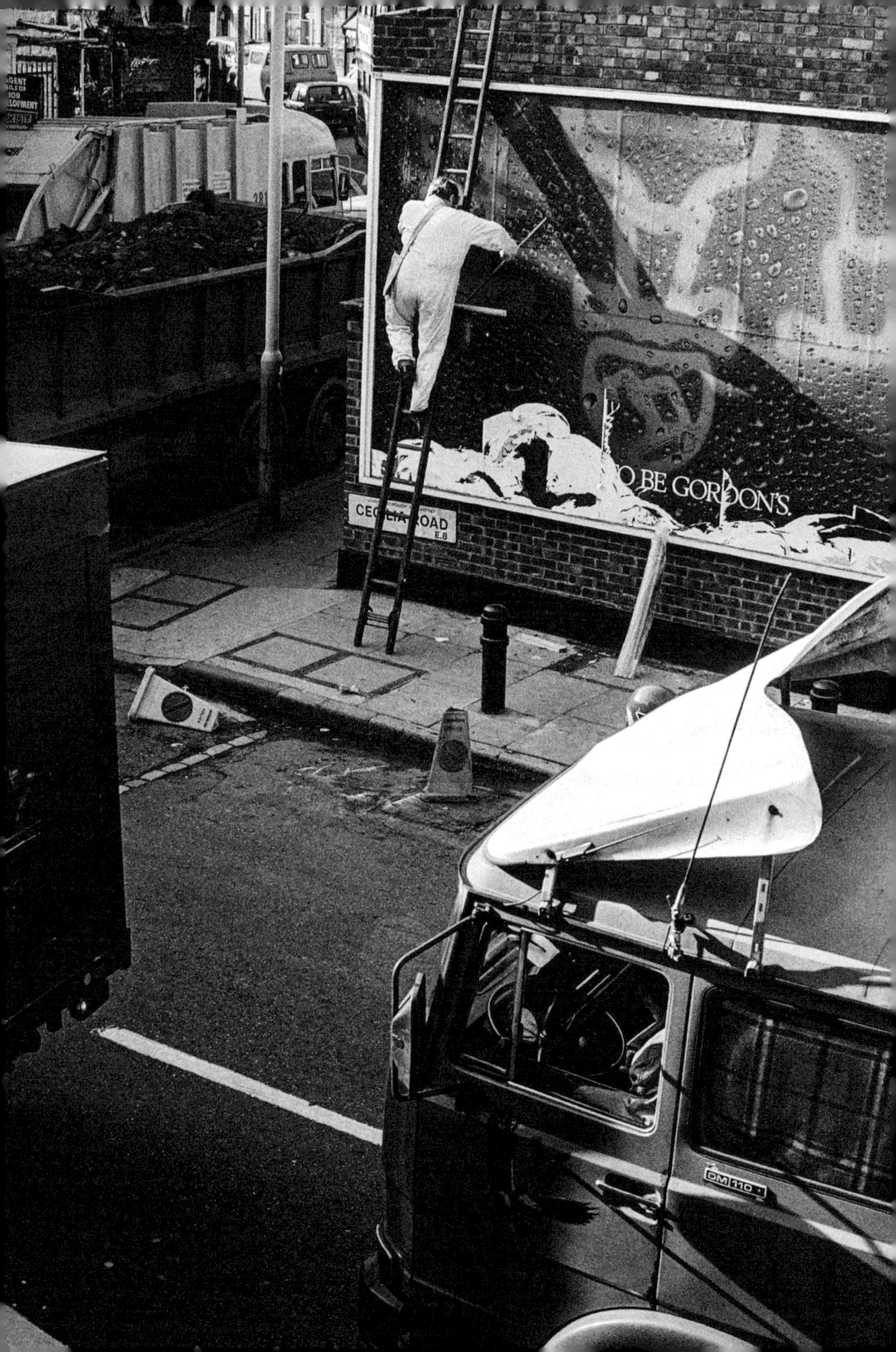
BE GORDON'S
CECILIA ROAD
E.8
OM 110

I spent a lot of time in the kitchen
looking out of the window,
waiting for the phone to ring and
feeling frustrated by lack of work.

Meanwhile my wife was busying
herself around Europe as a model.

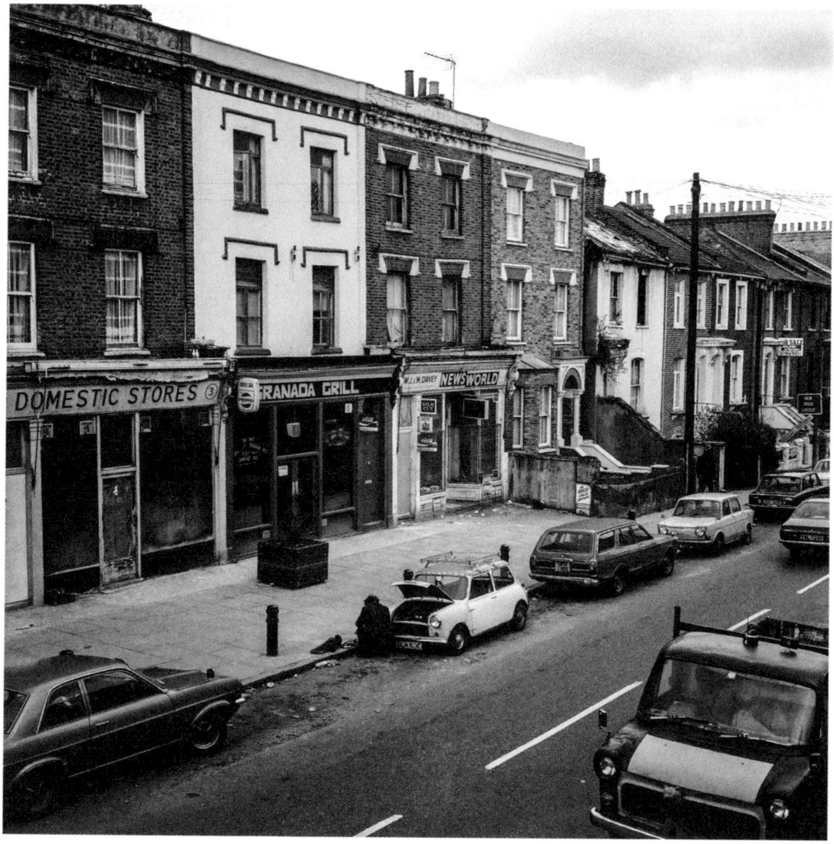

I kept seeing this bloke tinkering under the bonnet of an old Mini.

I was told he was from the Eastern Bloc.

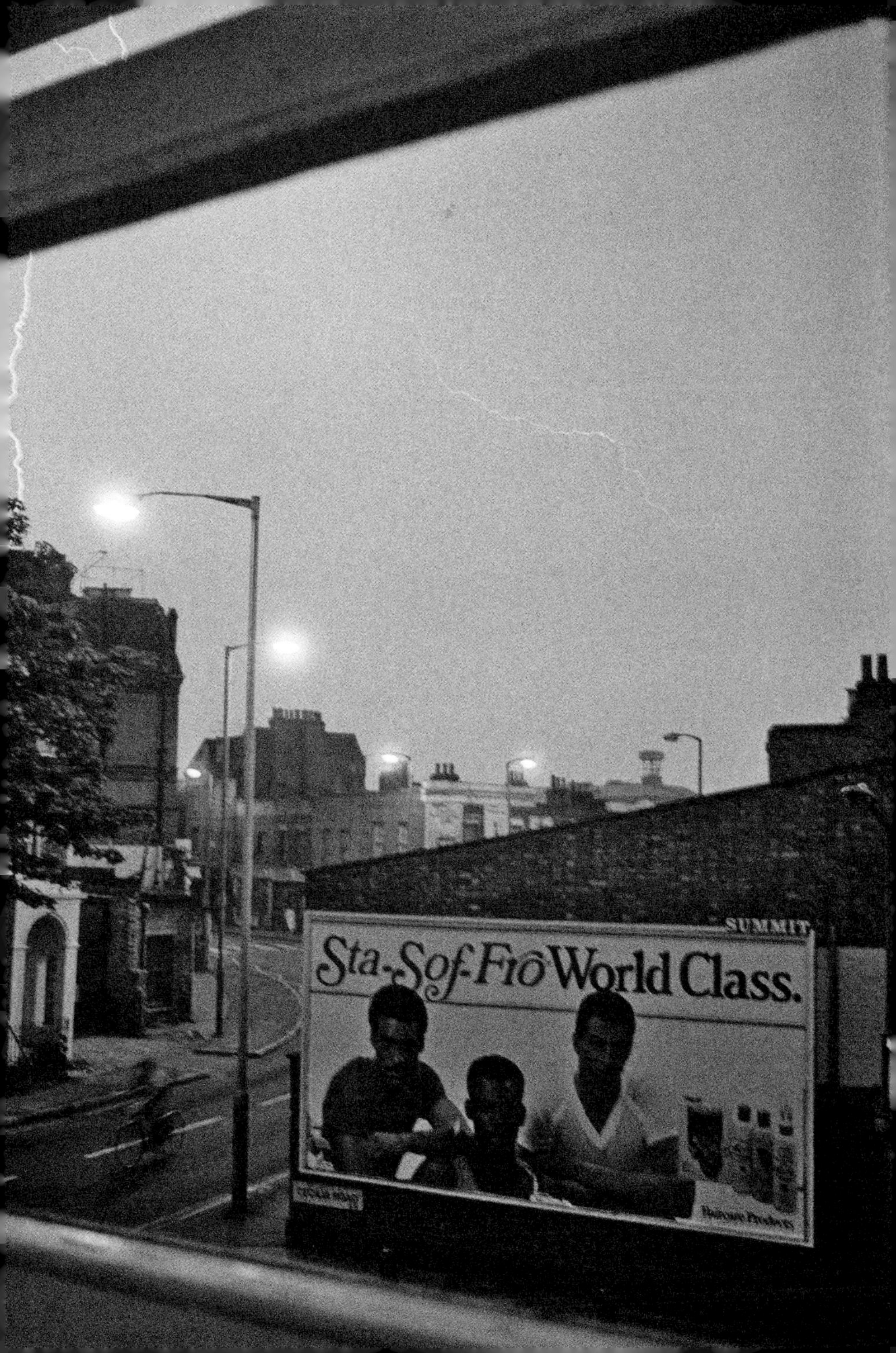
SUMMIT
Sta-Sof-Fro World Class.

One Evening I saw Prince Philip
on the other side of the road.

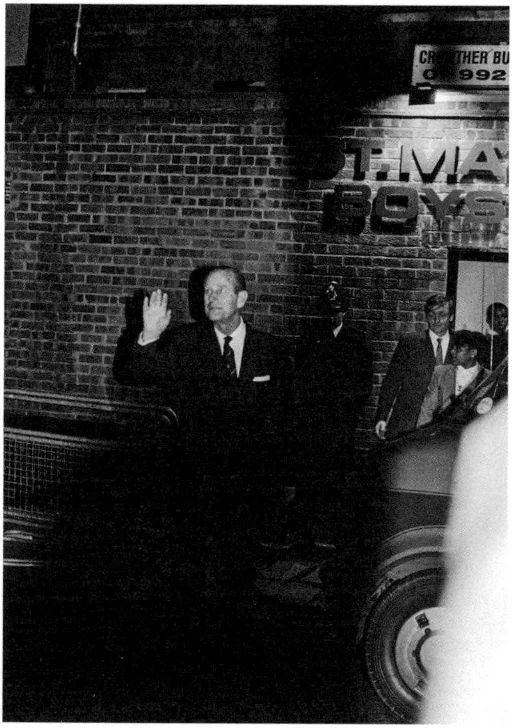

I grabbed my camera and
dashed downstairs
and before he disappeared,

I got a shot of him
waving to a group of Dalston Ladies.

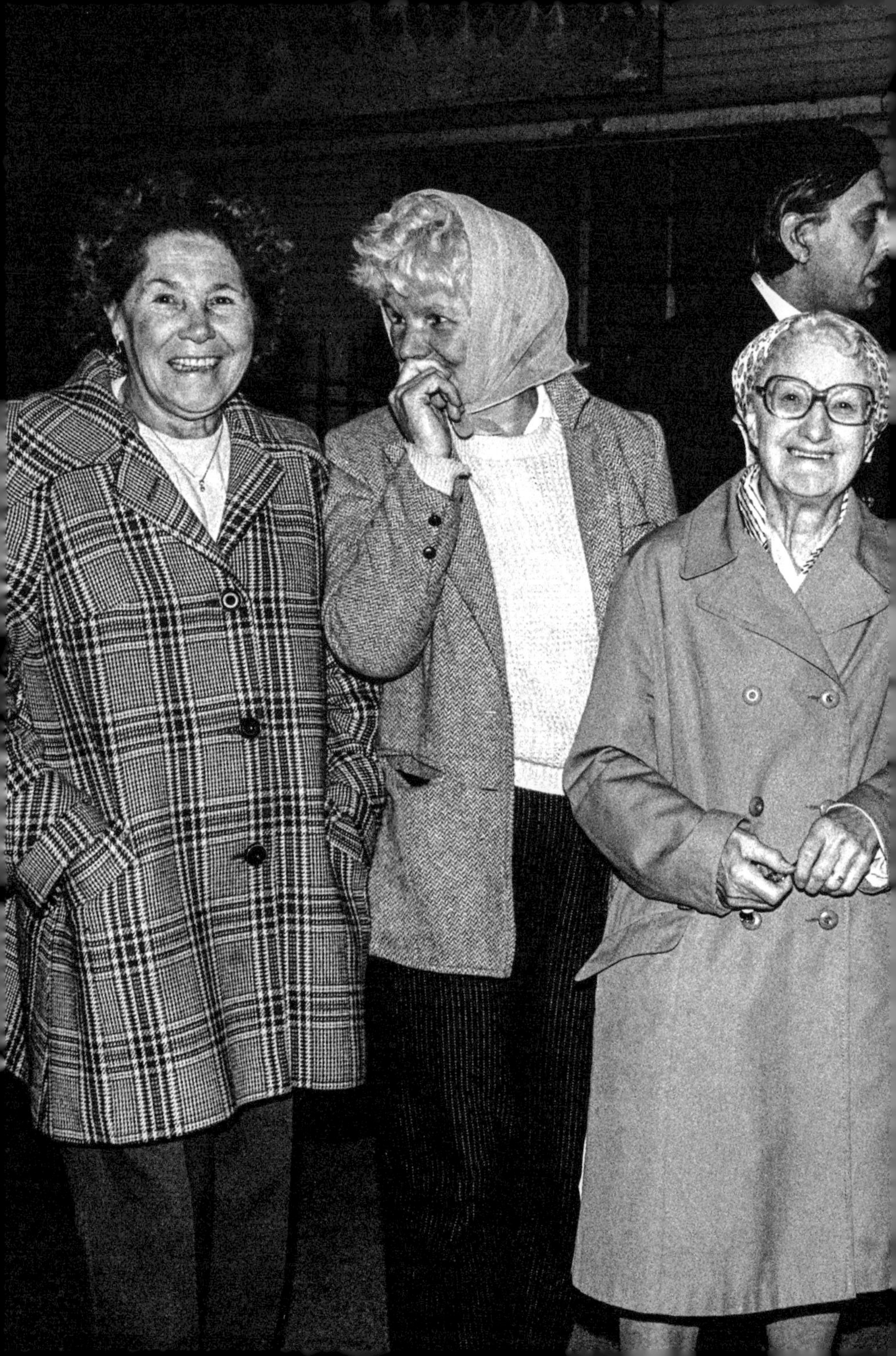

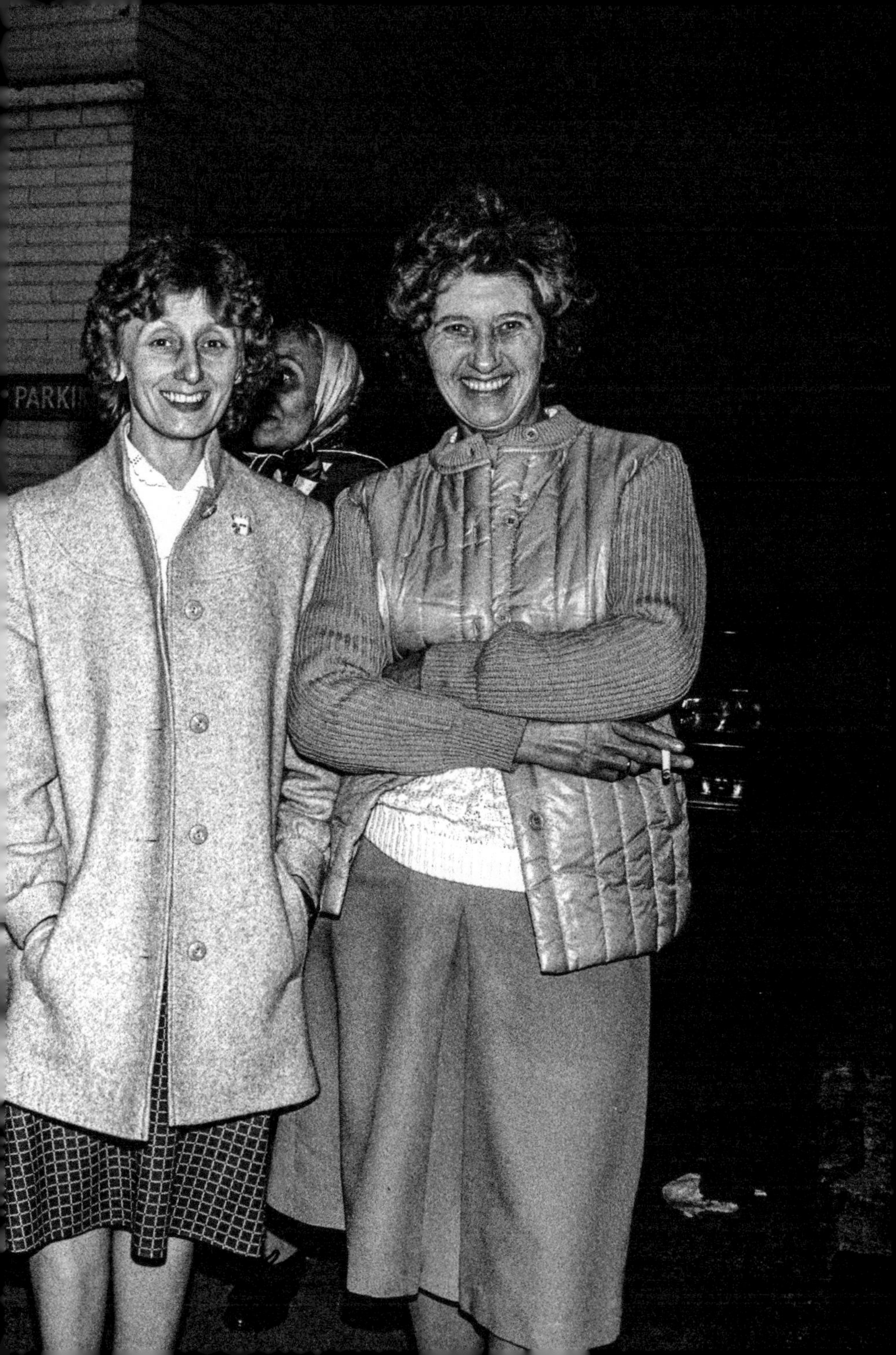

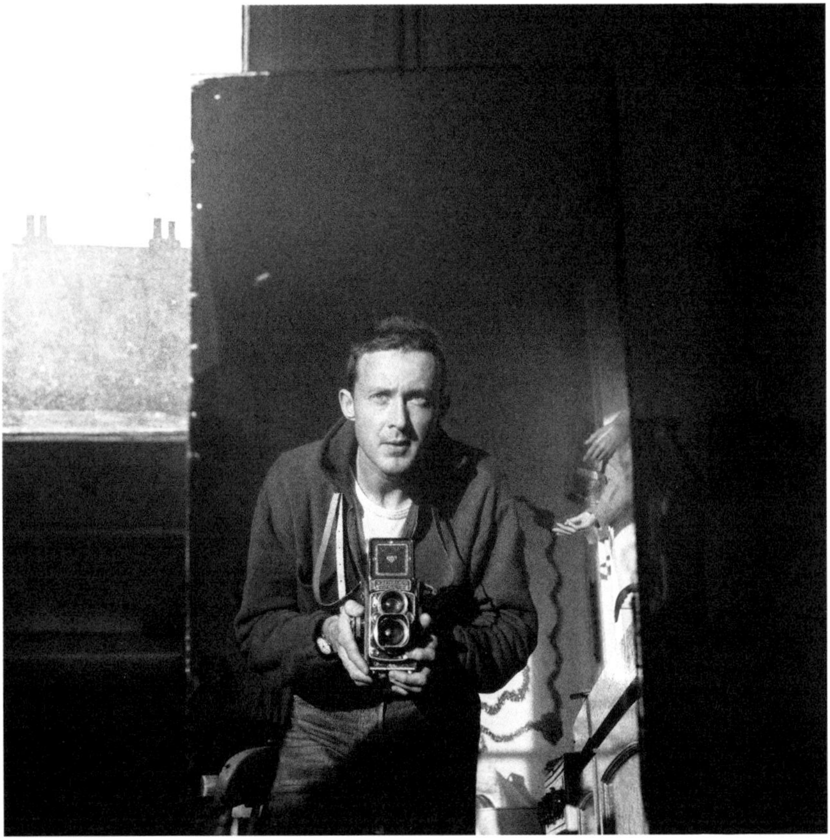

Royalty might have got me out
onto the street but it was
those smiling faces that inspired me.

I had changed city, changed continent,
now it was time to change my photography.

Fashion seemed too predictable.
So I bought an old 1950s Rolleiflex 2.8E2
camera and went out onto the street.

It took just one small step
to meet mankind in all its forms.

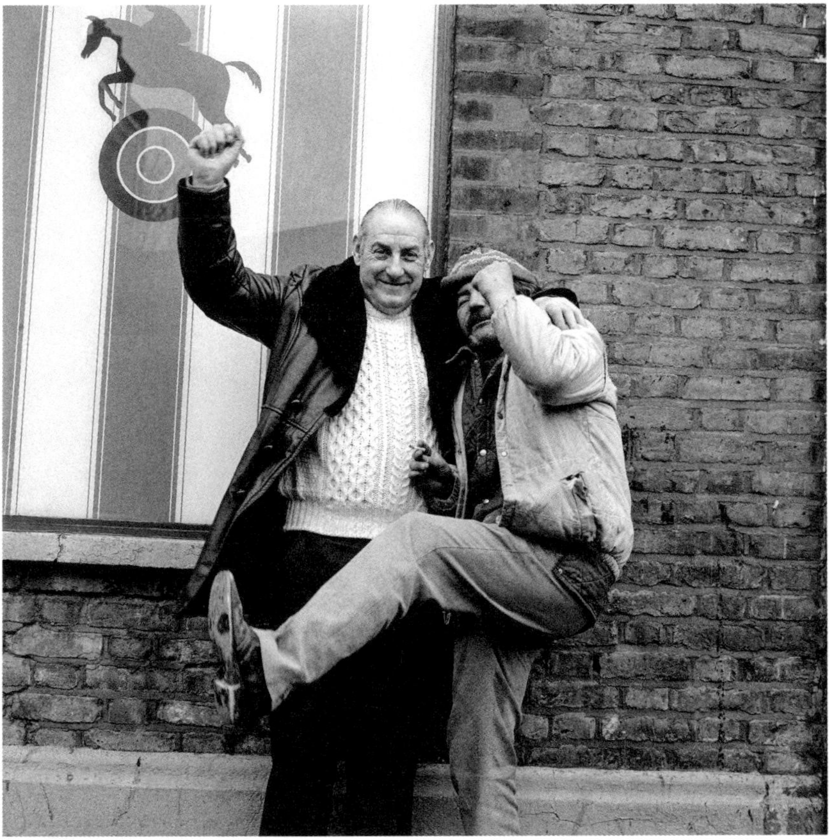

Winners on the razz outside the bookies.

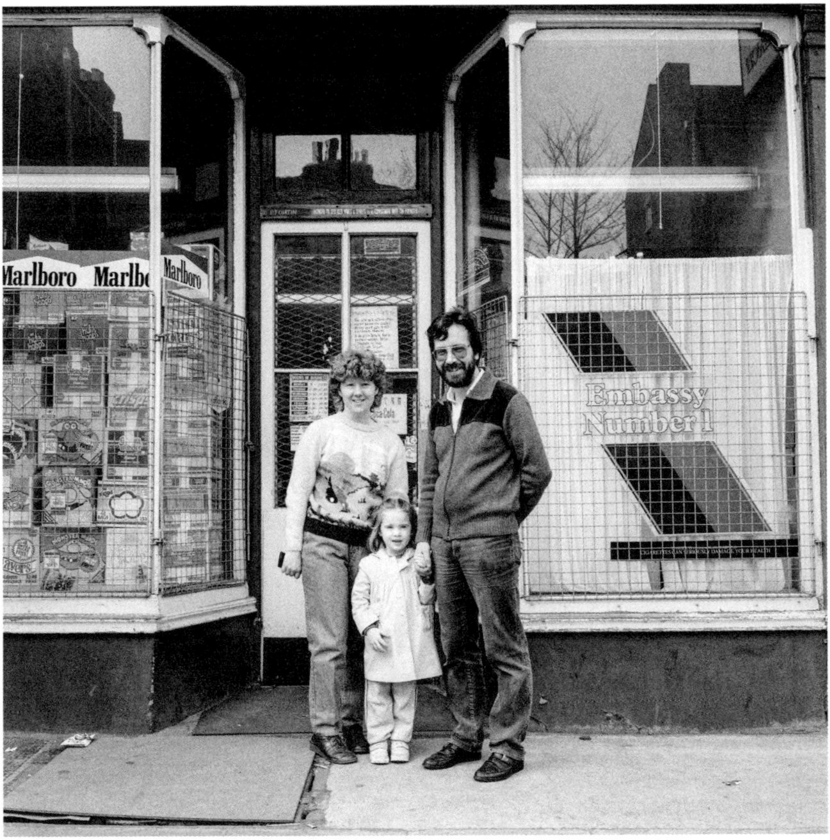

Danny in front of his off-license
"The Royal George" with his wife and kid.
(I never did ask him if the Prince
had popped in on his visit
to the Boys Club next door)

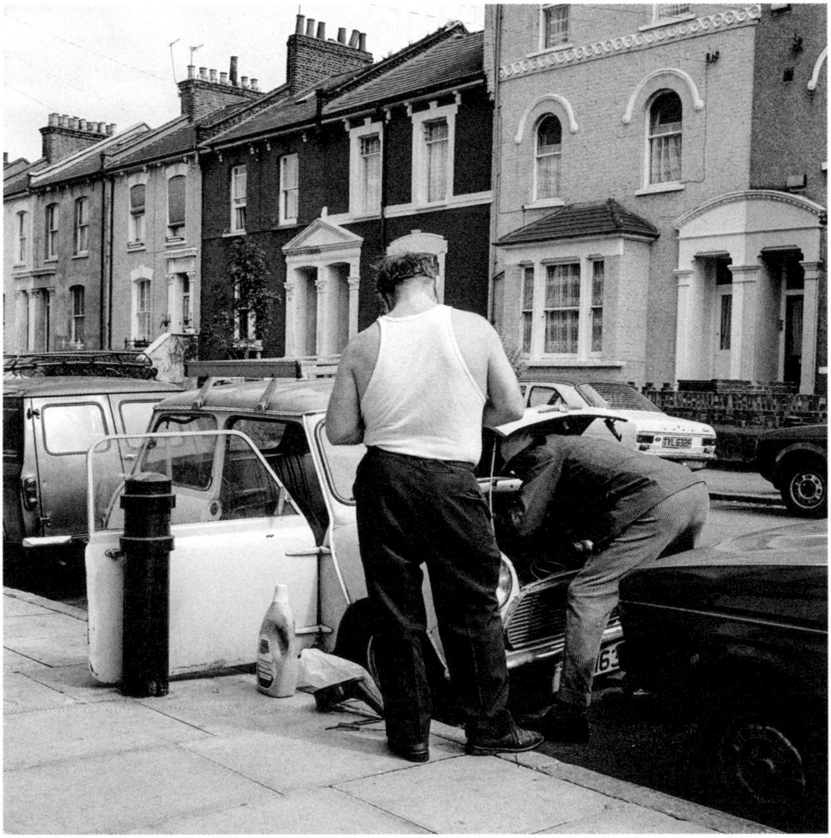
TYL 632F

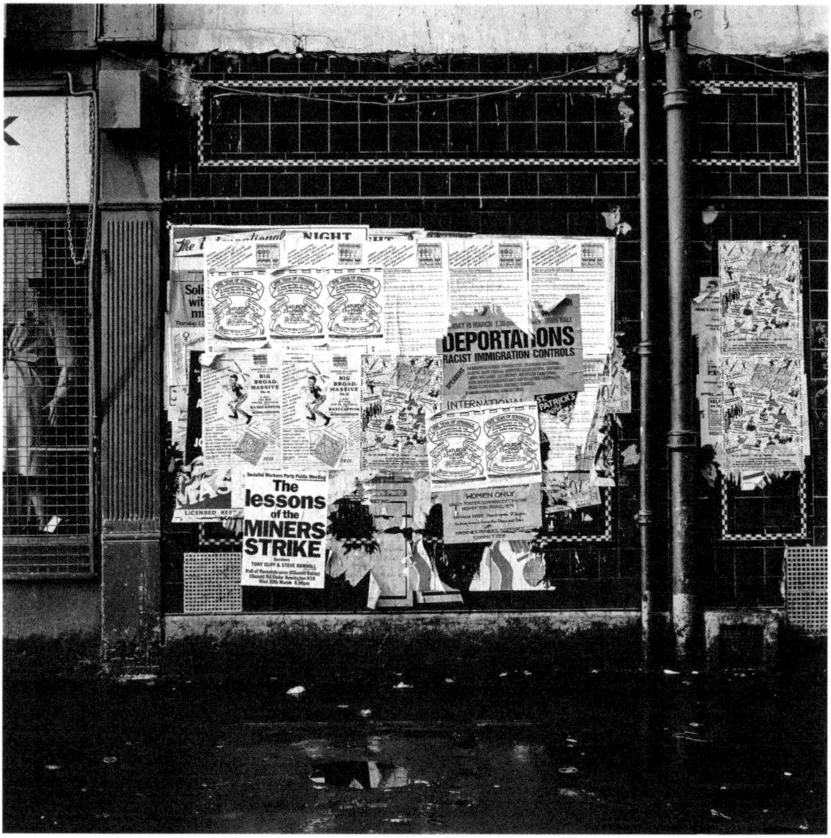
NIGHT
DEPORTATIONS
RACIST IMMIGRATION CONTROLS
INTERNATIONAL
ST. PATRICK'S
BIG BROAD-MASSIVE
Socialist Workers Party Public Meeting
The lessons of the MINERS STRIKE
WOMEN ONLY
LICENSED

It was Thatcher's Britain:
the miners strike had just started
and the demise of the GLC was looming.

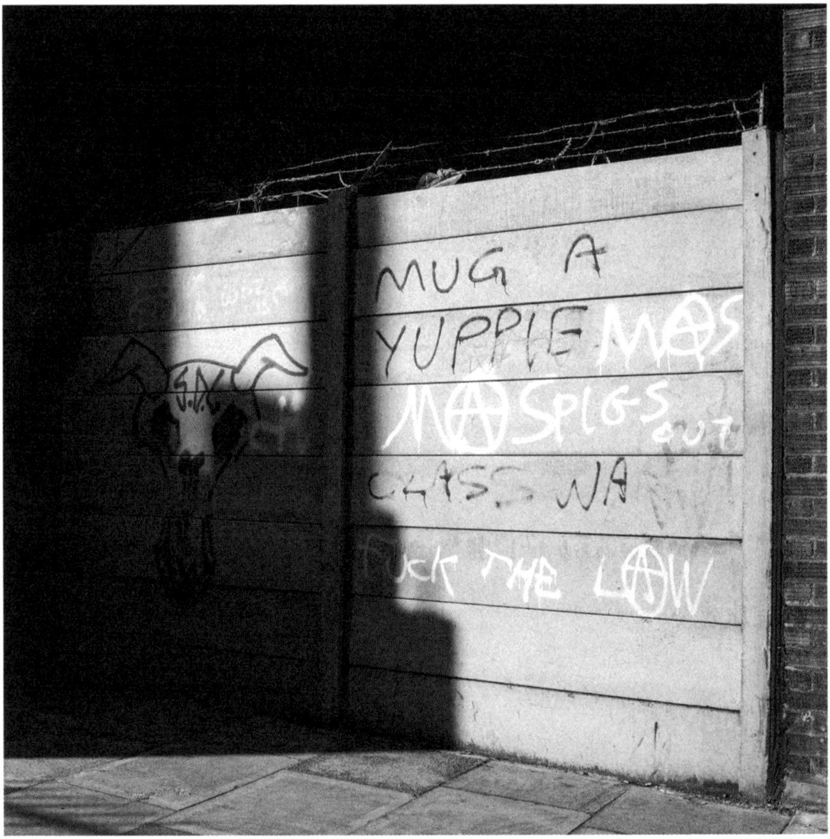

There were Cabbage Patch dolls in
young girls' arms and Yuppies were
a new threatening breed.

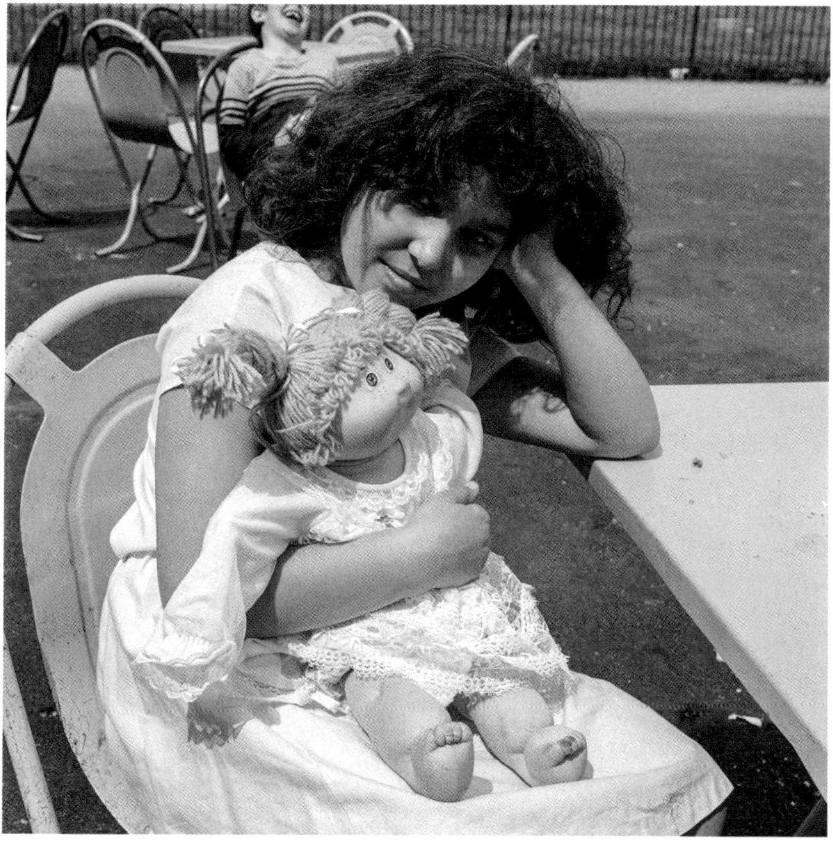

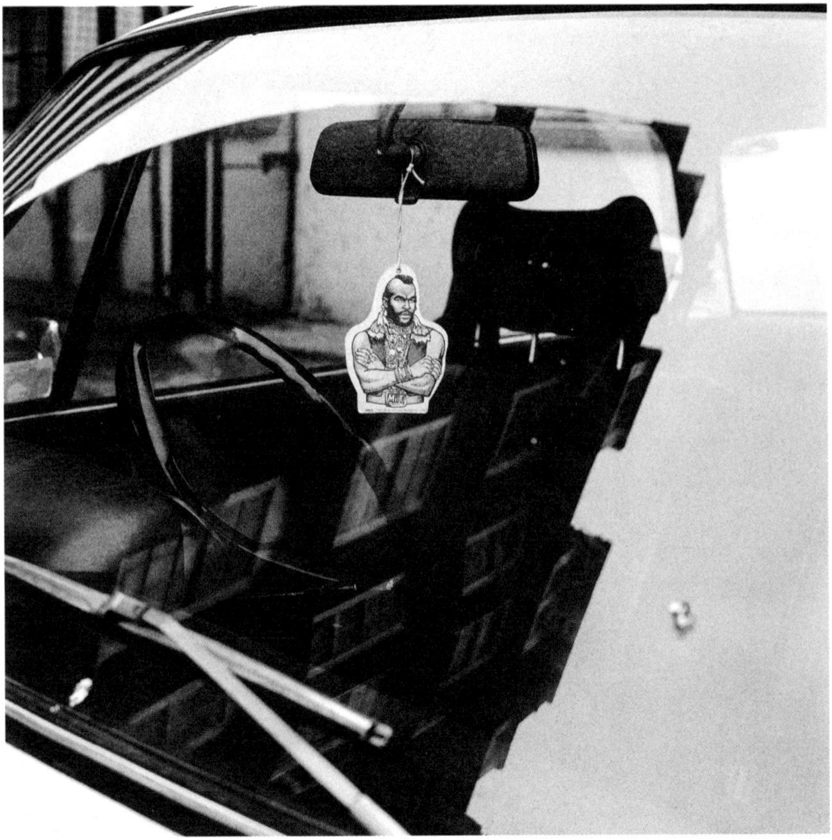

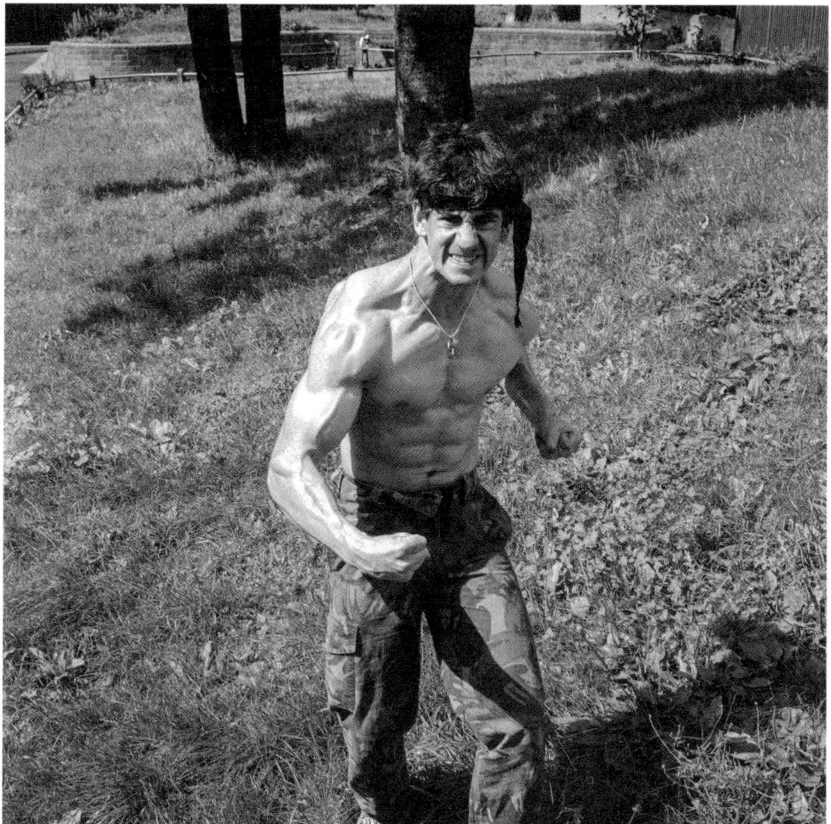

Rambo and Mr.T were the action heroes while on the streets the anti-apartheid movement was gaining momentum and the BNP had newly formed.

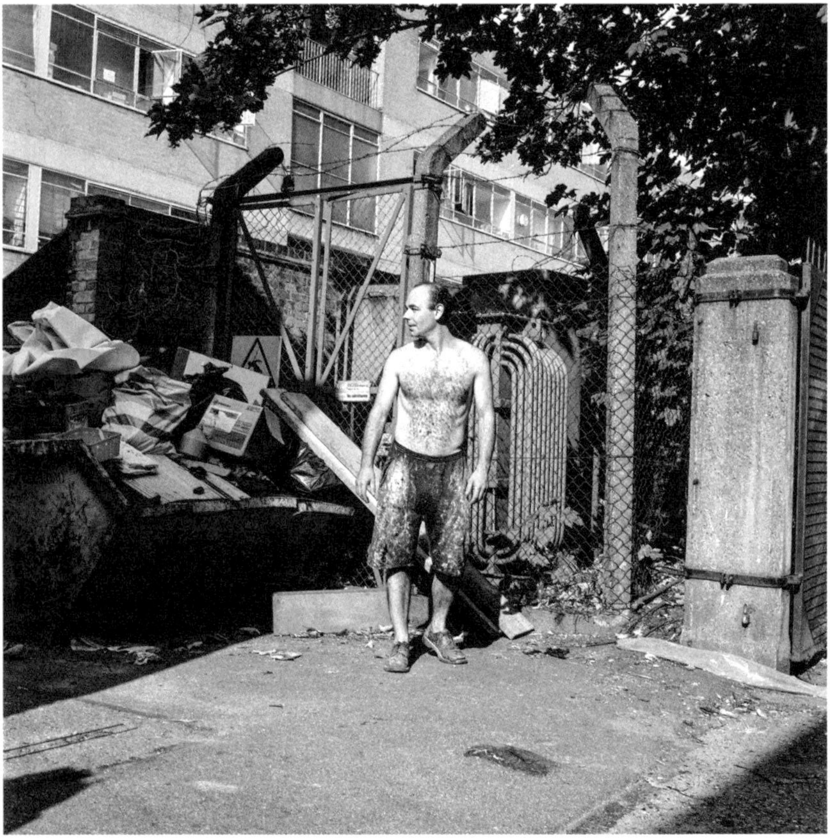

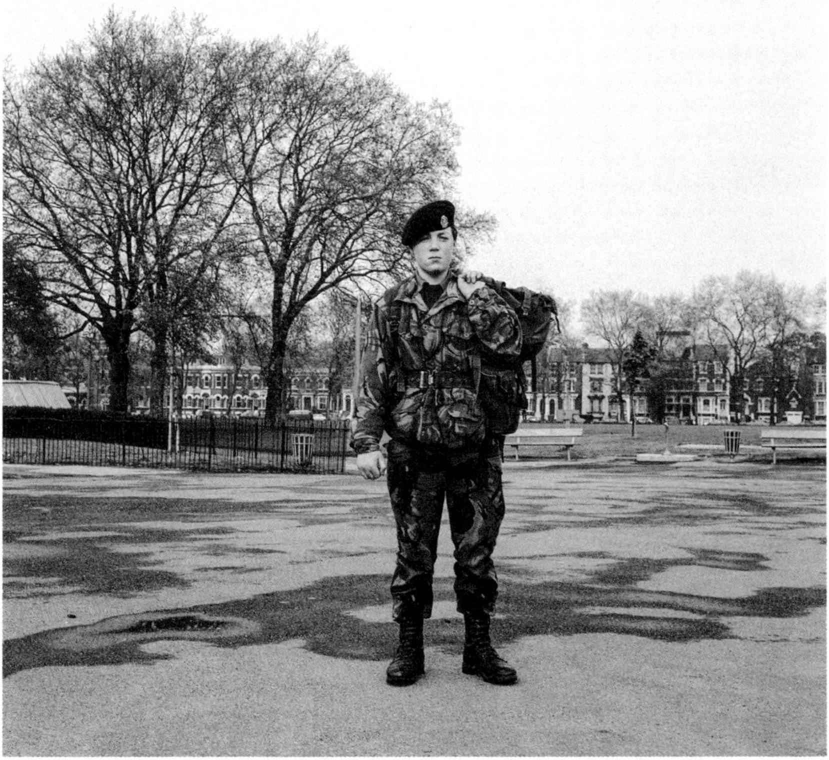

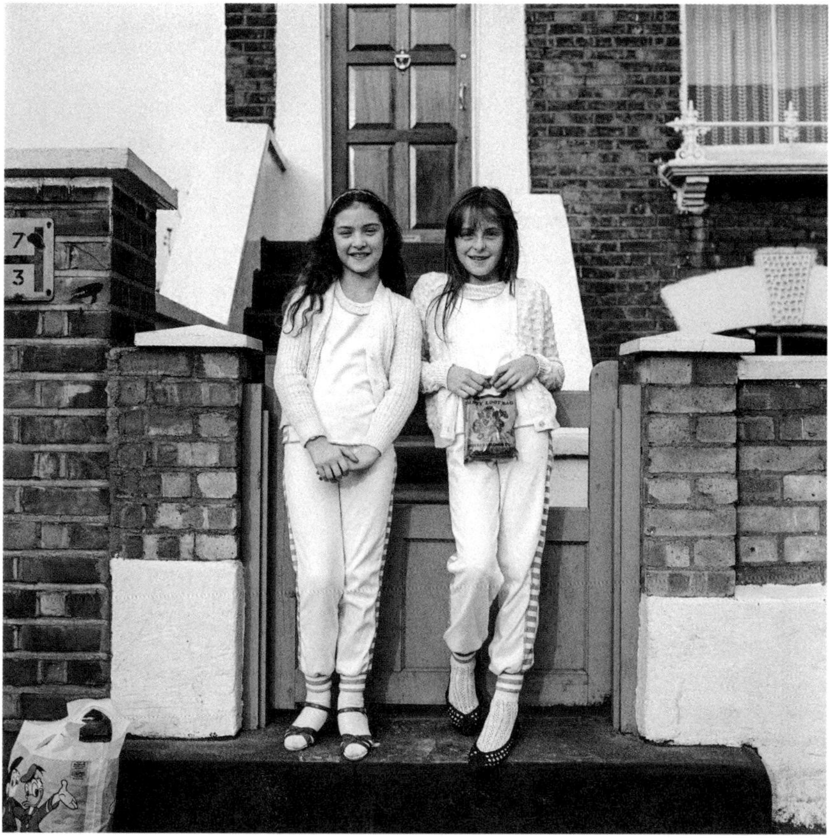

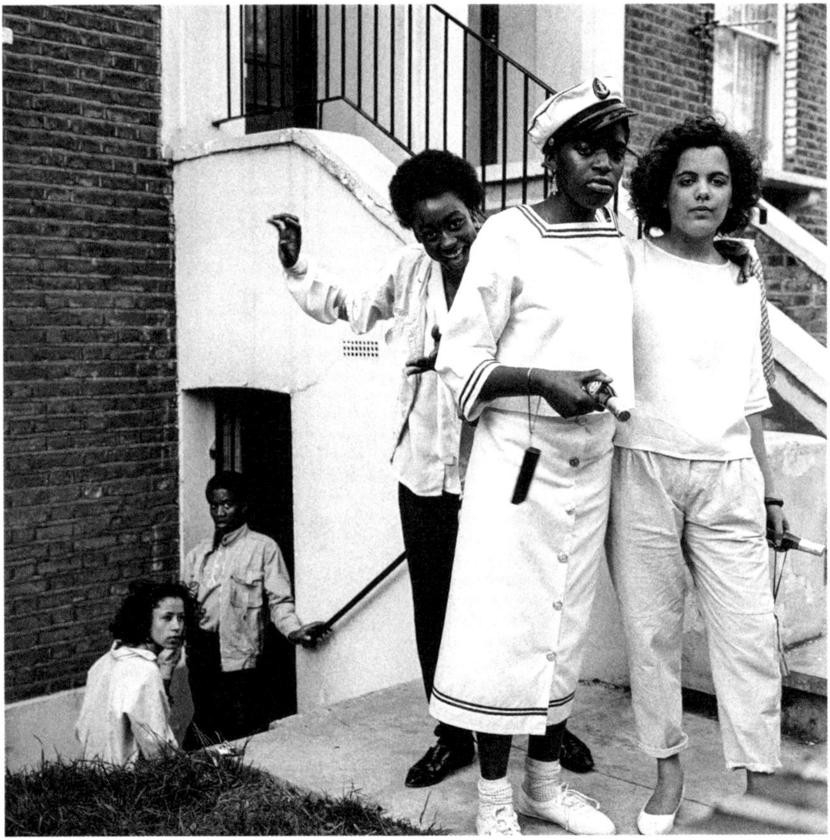

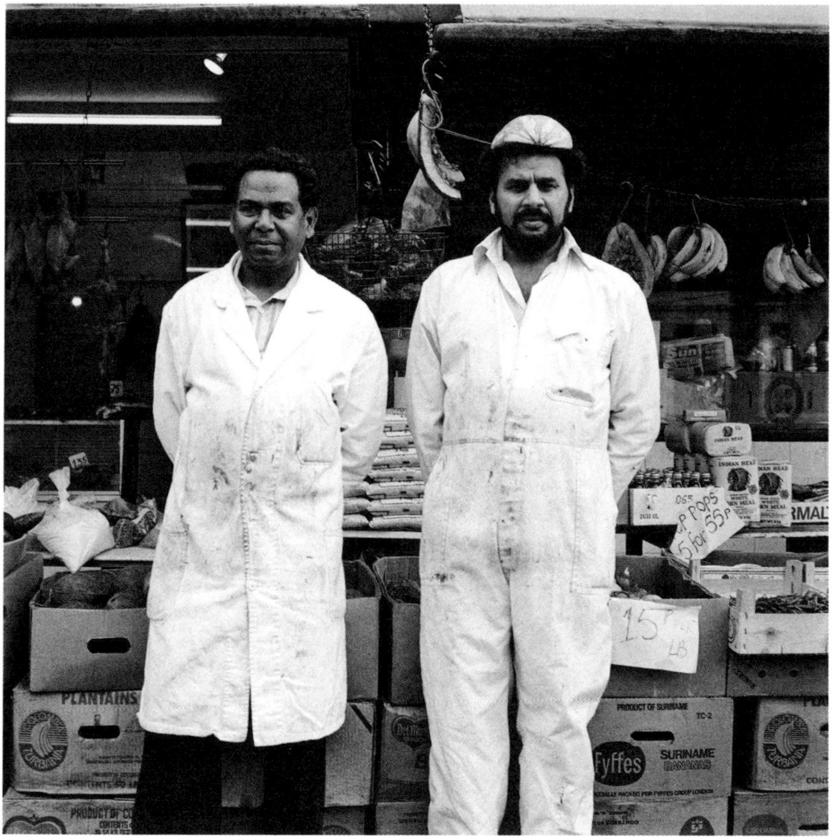

PLANTAINS
INDIAN HEAD
5 for 55p
15p
LB
PRODUCT OF SURINAME
TC-2
Fyffes
SURINAME
BANANAS

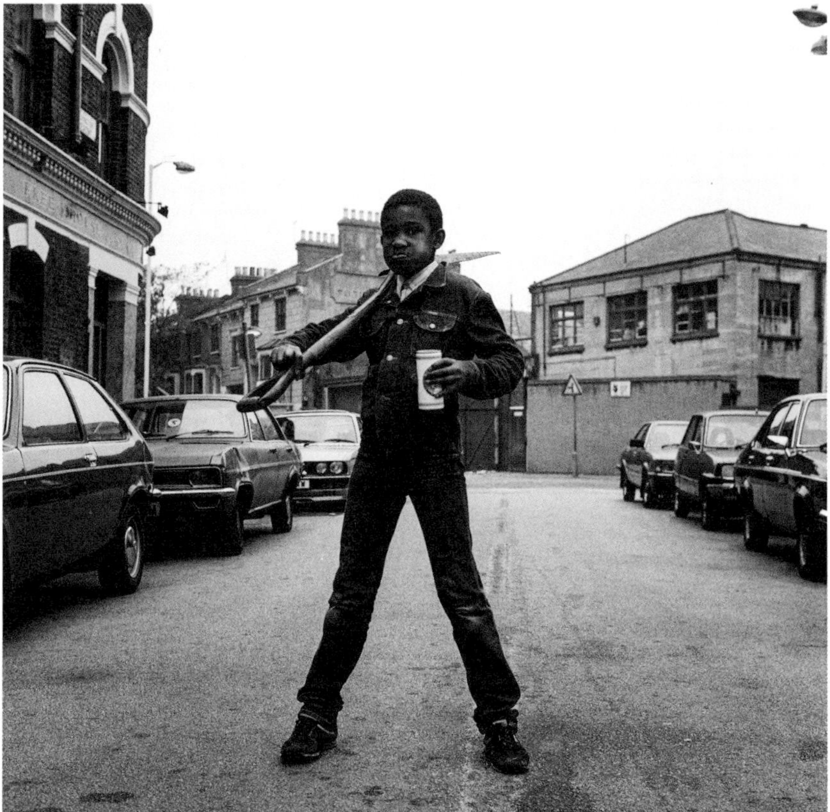

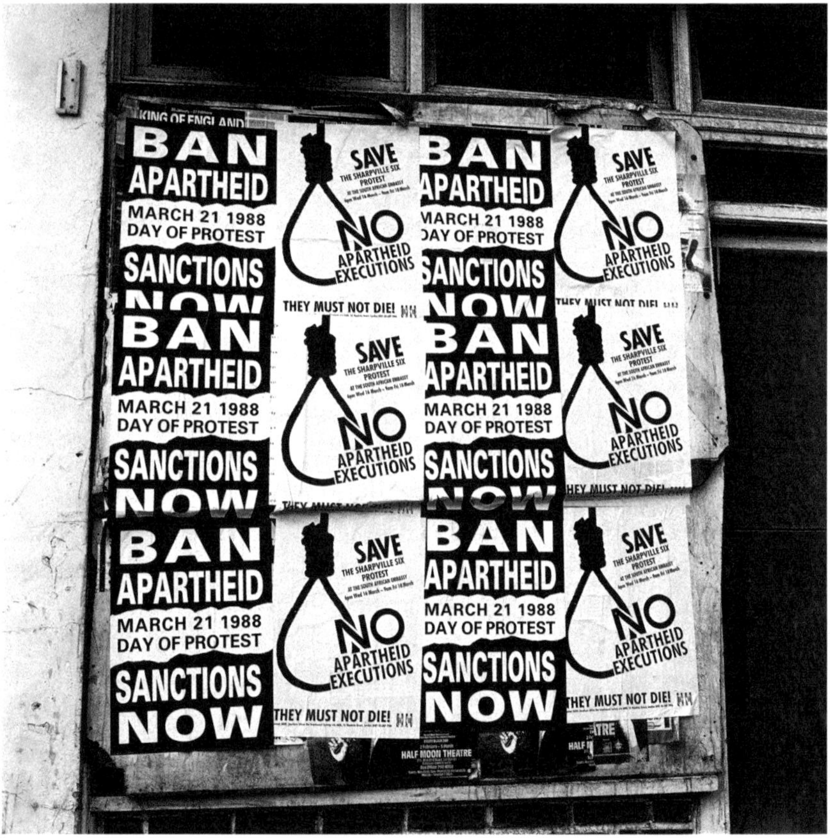
KING OF ENGLAND
BAN
APARTHEID
MARCH 21 1988
DAY OF PROTEST
SANCTIONS
NOW
SAVE
THE SHARPVILLE SIX
PROTEST
NO
APARTHEID
EXECUTIONS
THEY MUST NOT DIE!
HALF MOON THEATRE

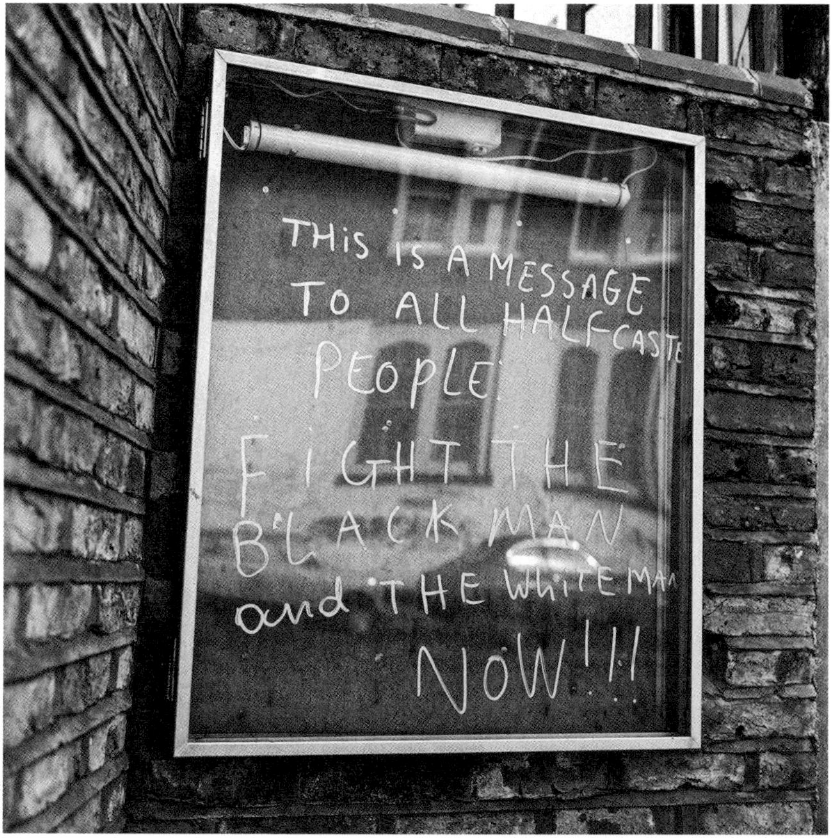
THIS IS A MESSAGE
TO ALL HALFCASTE
PEOPLE:
FIGHT THE
BLACK MAN
and THE WHITE MAN
NOW!!!

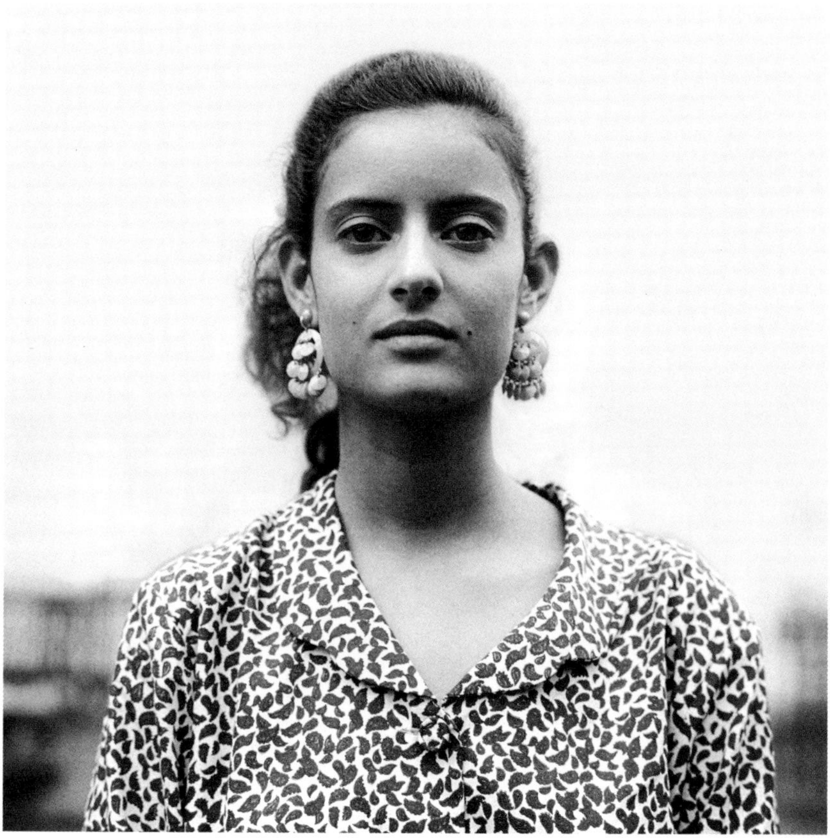

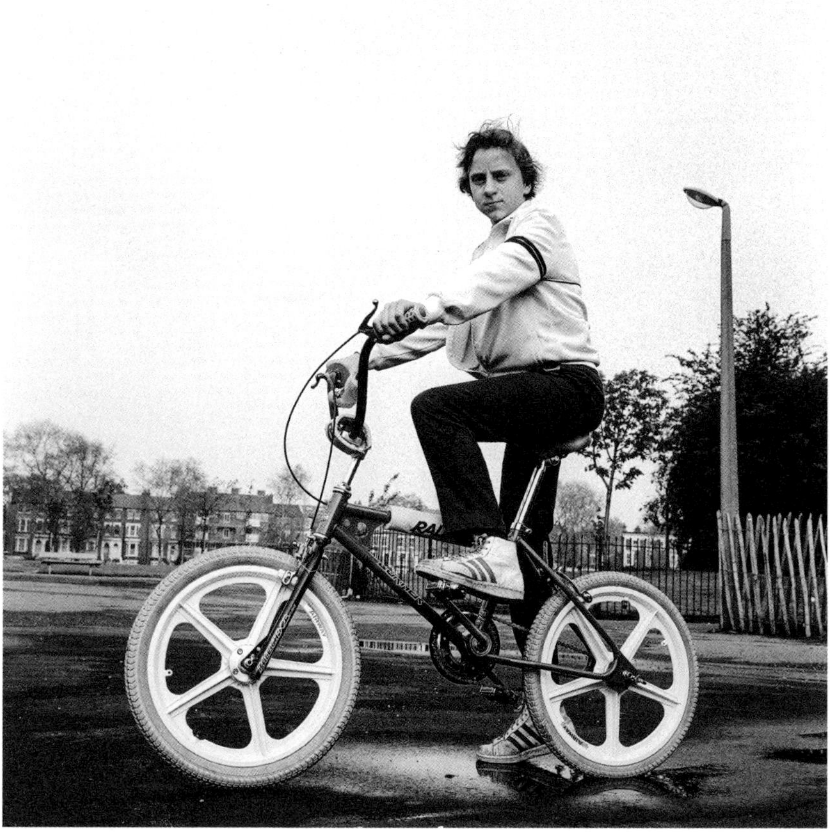

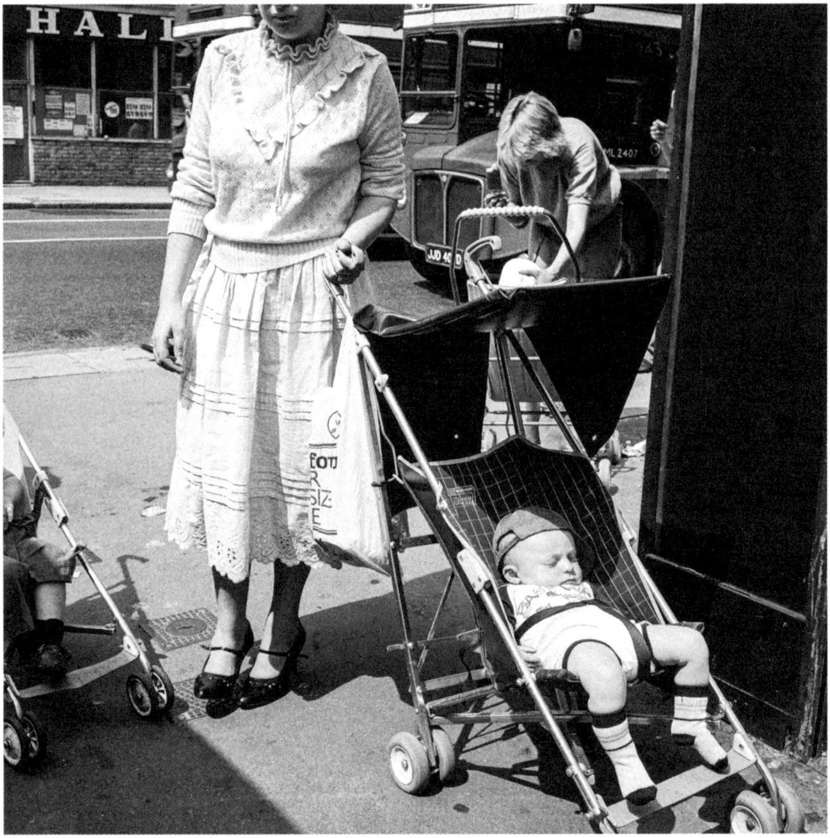

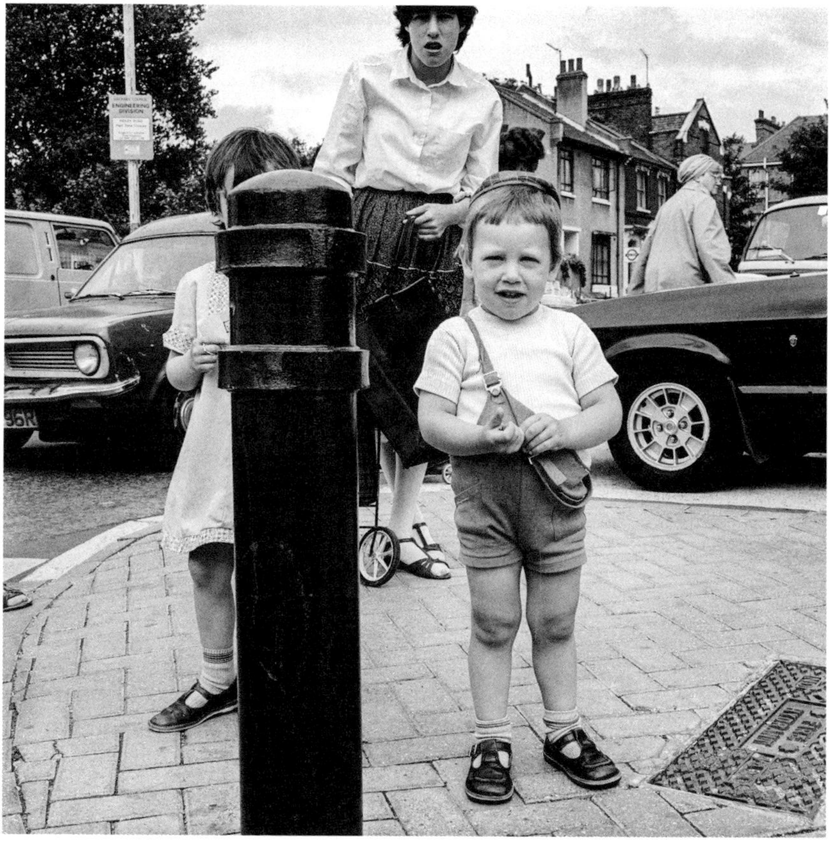

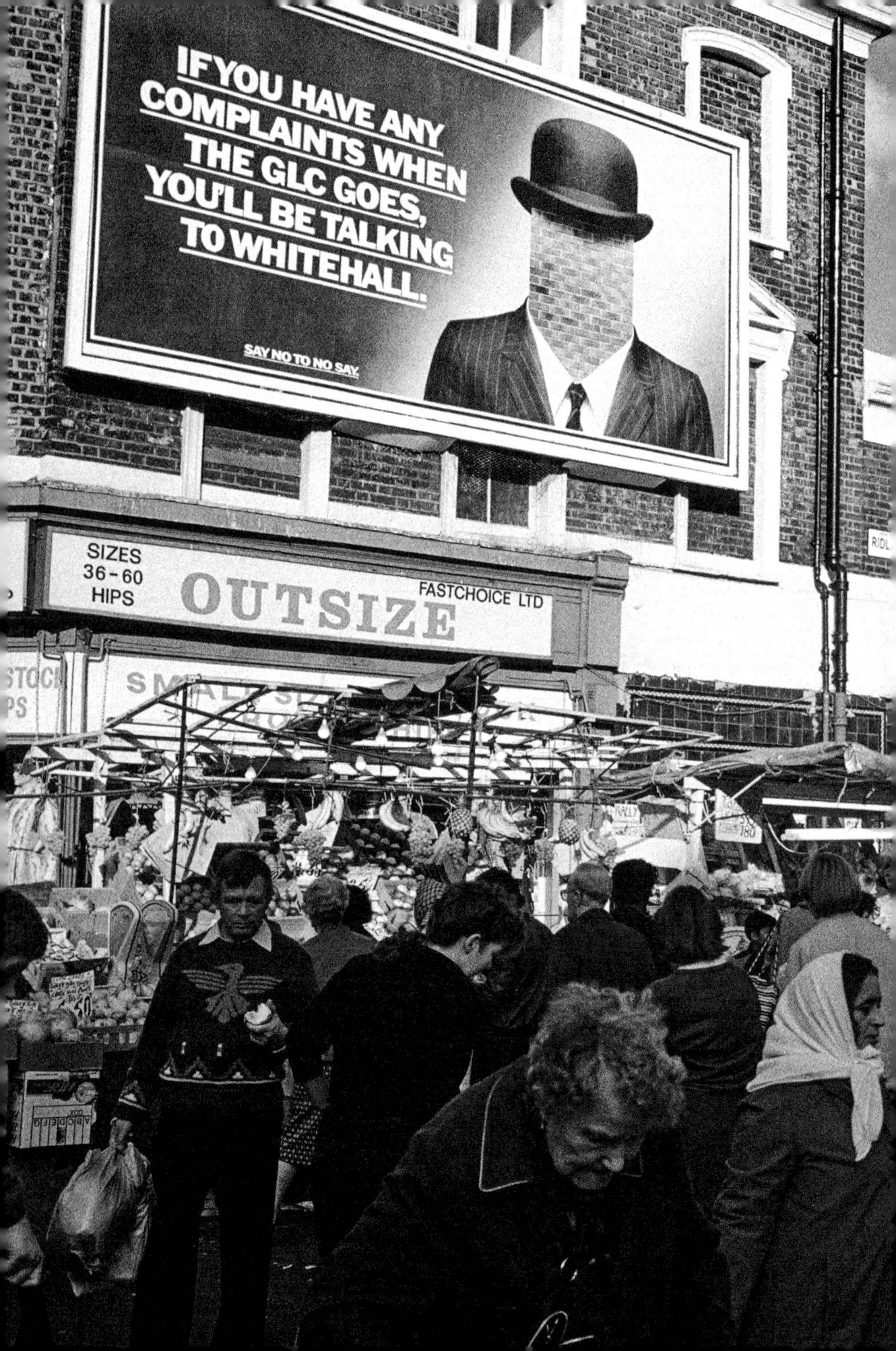
IF YOU HAVE ANY COMPLAINTS WHEN THE GLC GOES, YOU'LL BE TALKING TO WHITEHALL.
SAY NO TO NO SAY.
SIZES 36-60 HIPS
OUTSIZE
FASTCHOICE LTD

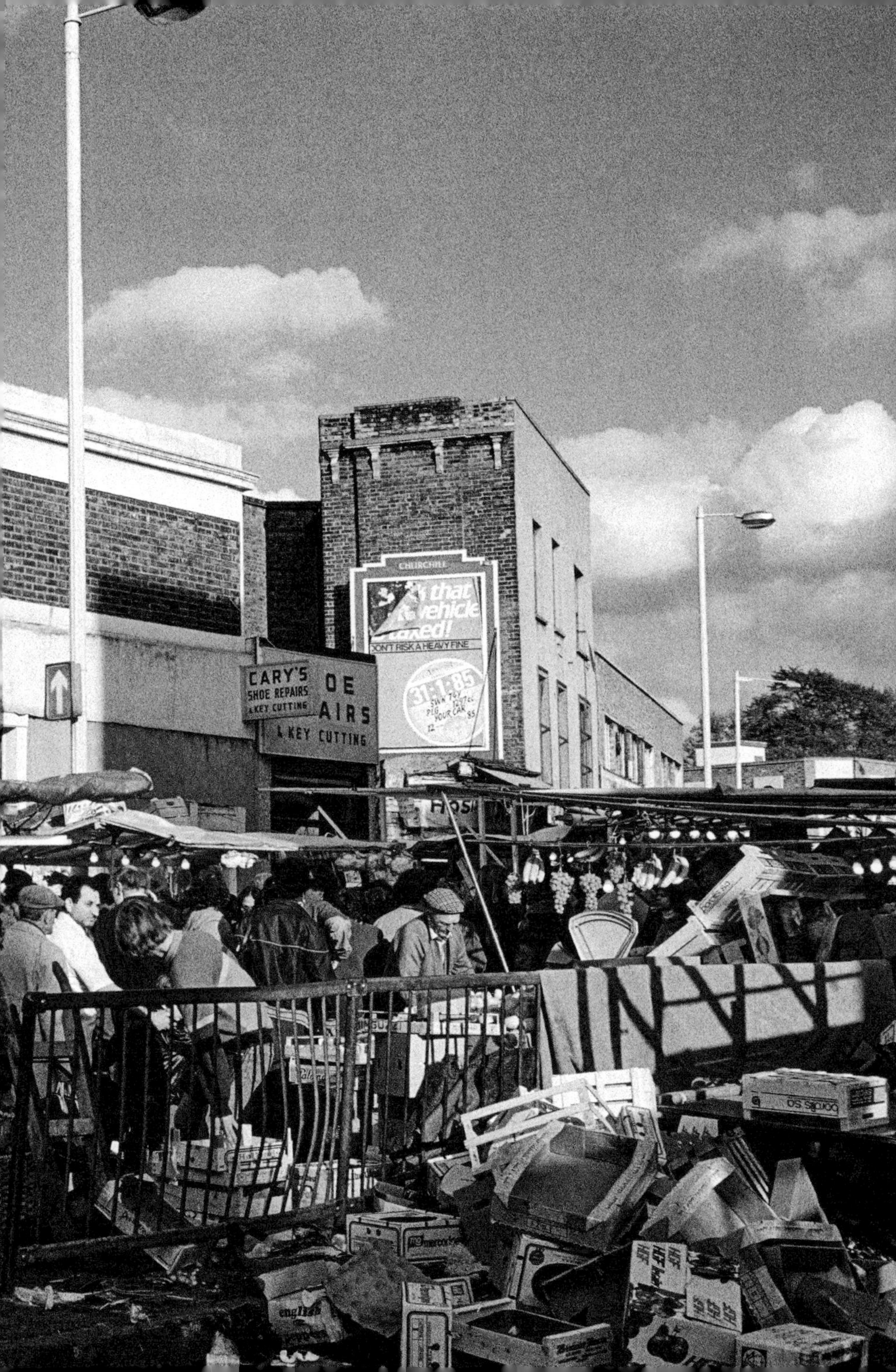
CARY'S
SHOE REPAIRS
& KEY CUTTING
OE
AIRS
& KEY CUTTING
CHURCHILL
DON'T RISK A HEAVY FINE
31-1-85

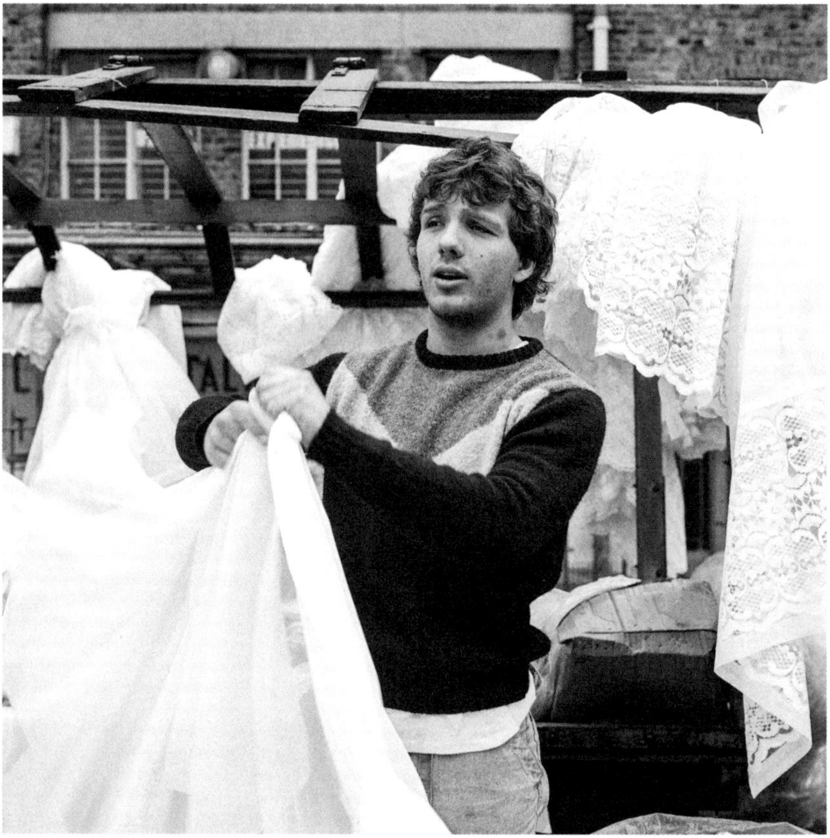

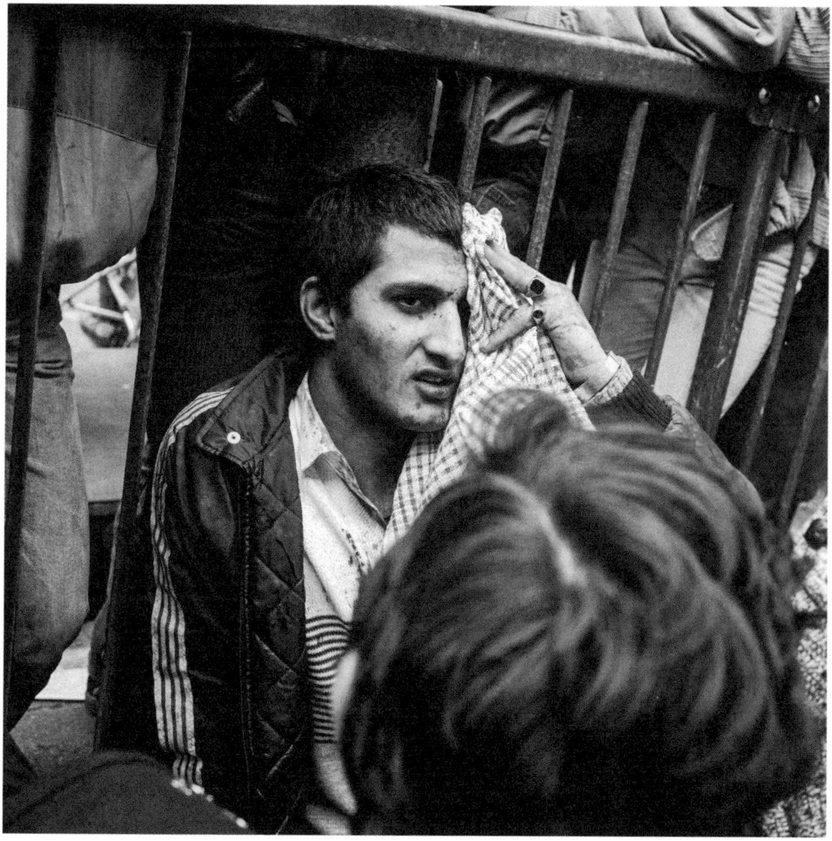

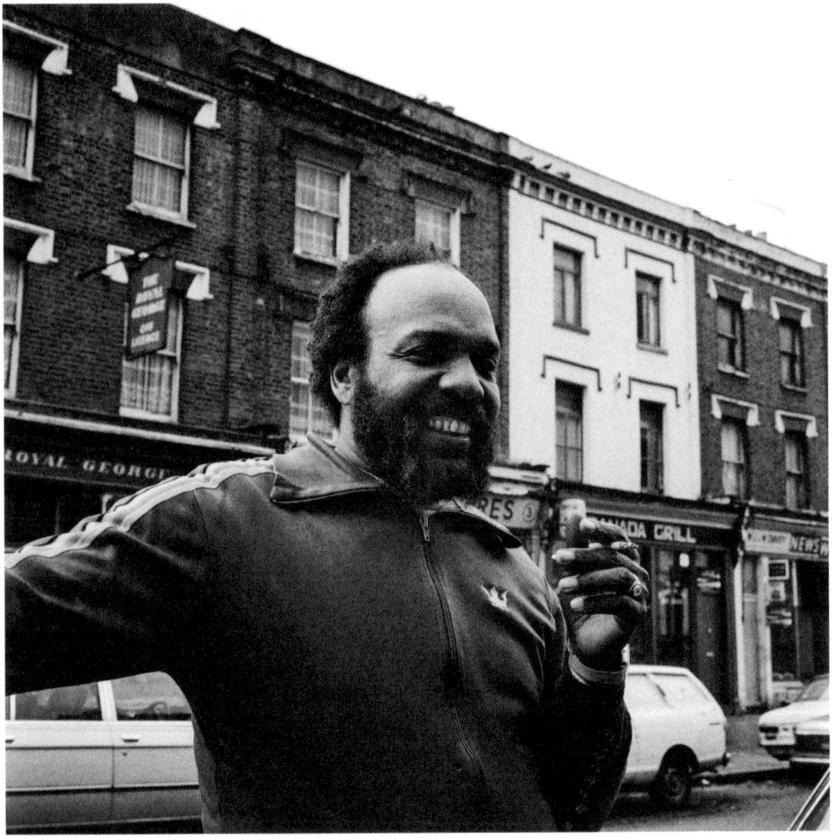

The one and only Rupie Edwards
whose record stall at the market
filled the air with sweet reggae tunes.

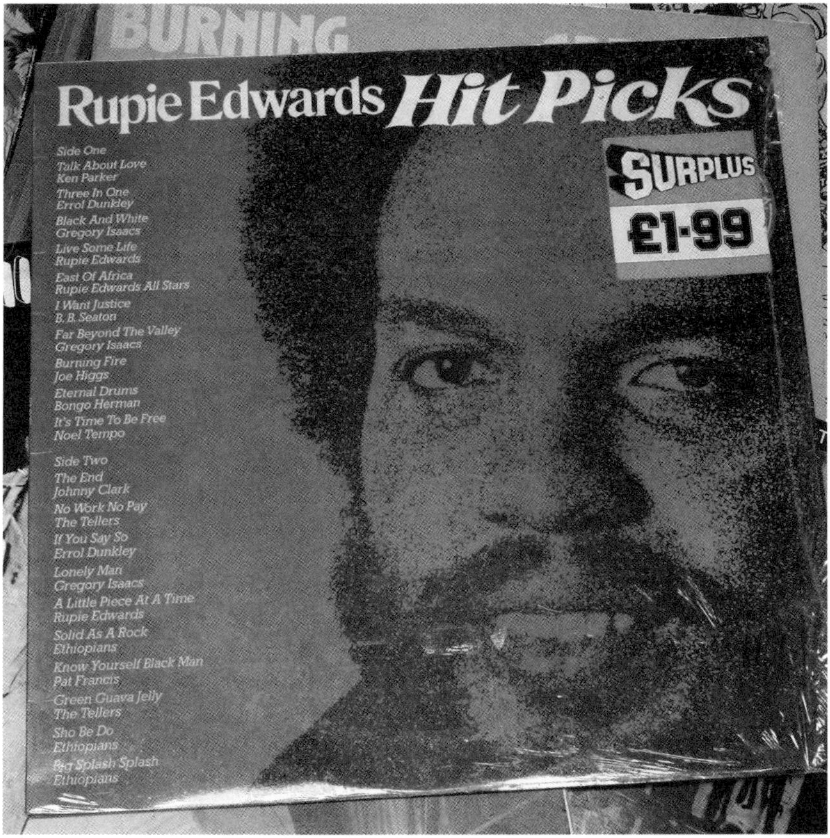

His 'Hit Picks' became the soundtrack
to my life in Dalston.

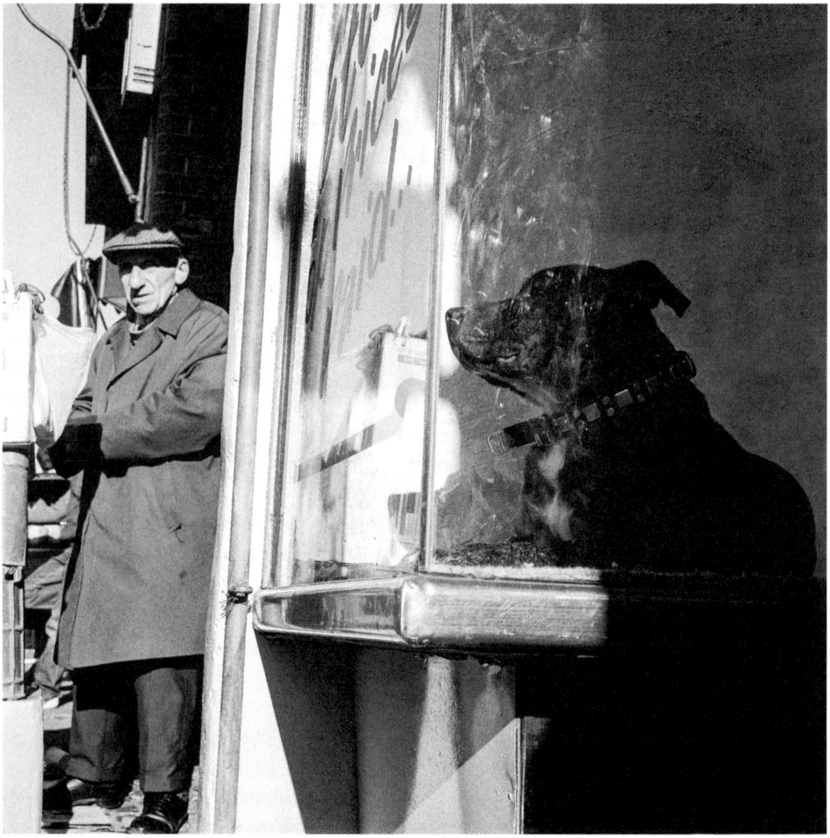

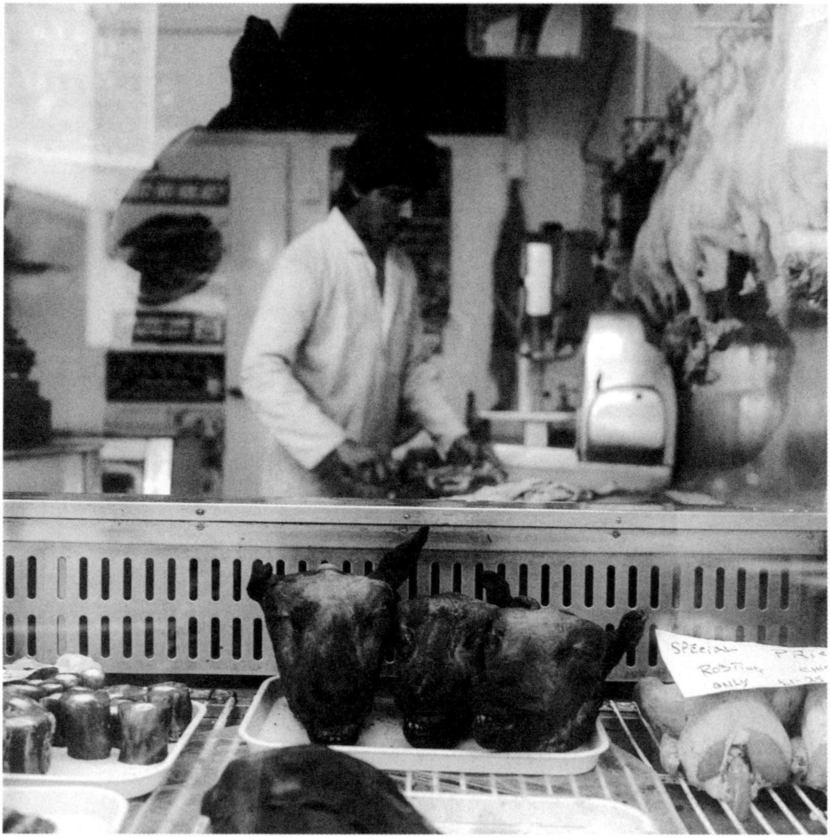
SPECIAL
ONLY

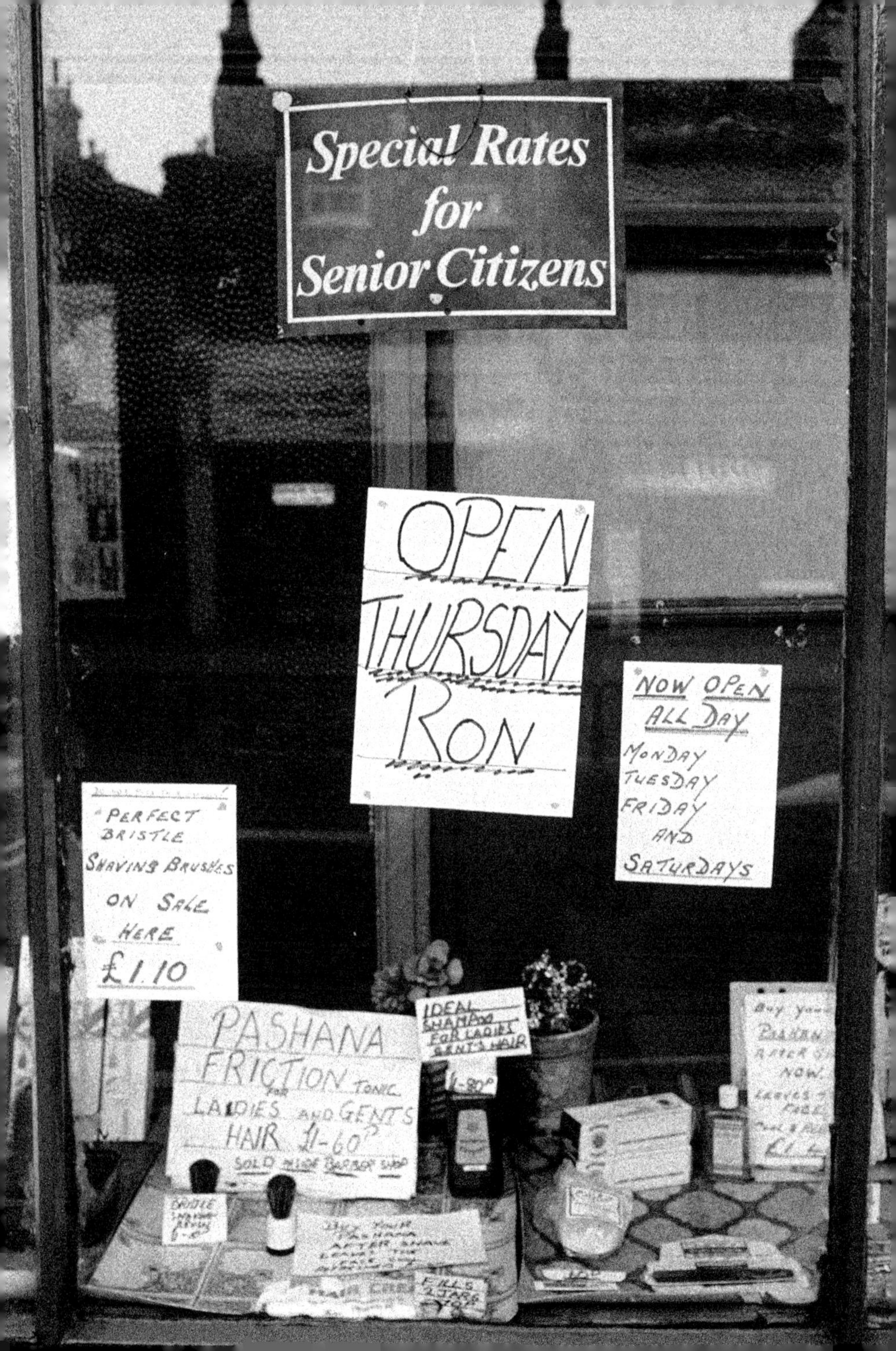
Special Rates for Senior Citizens
OPEN THURSDAY RON
NOW OPEN ALL DAY MONDAY TUESDAY FRIDAY AND SATURDAYS
PERFECT BRISTLE SHAVING BRUSHES ON SALE HERE £1.10
PASHANA FRICTION TONIC FOR LADIES AND GENTS HAIR £1-60P
IDEAL SHAMPOO FOR LADIES GENT'S HAIR

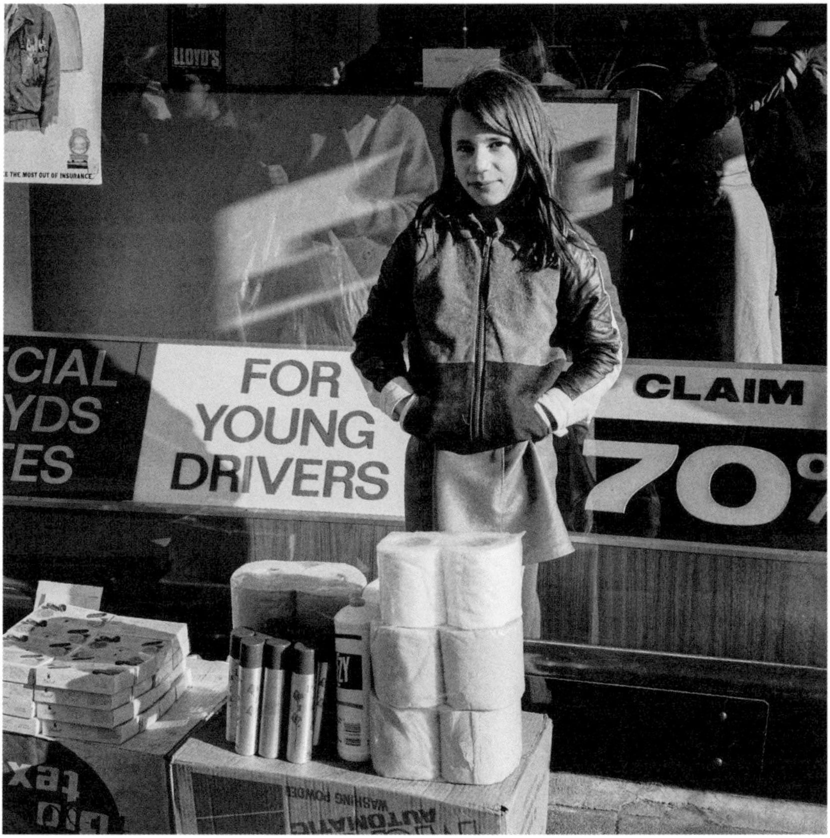

LLOYD'S
THE MOST OUT OF INSURANCE
CIAL
YDS
TES
FOR
YOUNG
DRIVERS
CLAIM
70%
WASHING POWDER

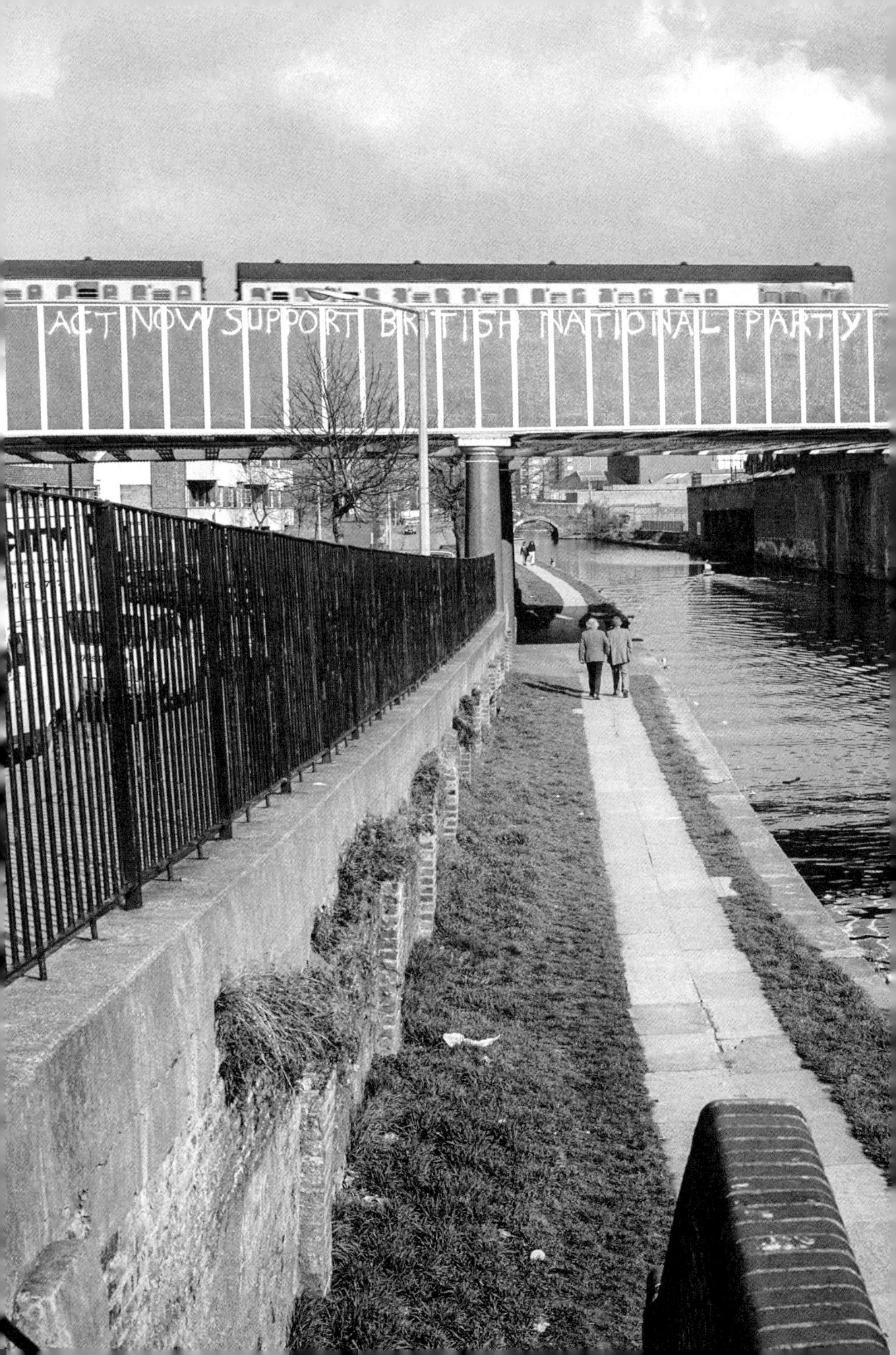
ACT NOW SUPPORT BRITISH NATIONAL PARTY

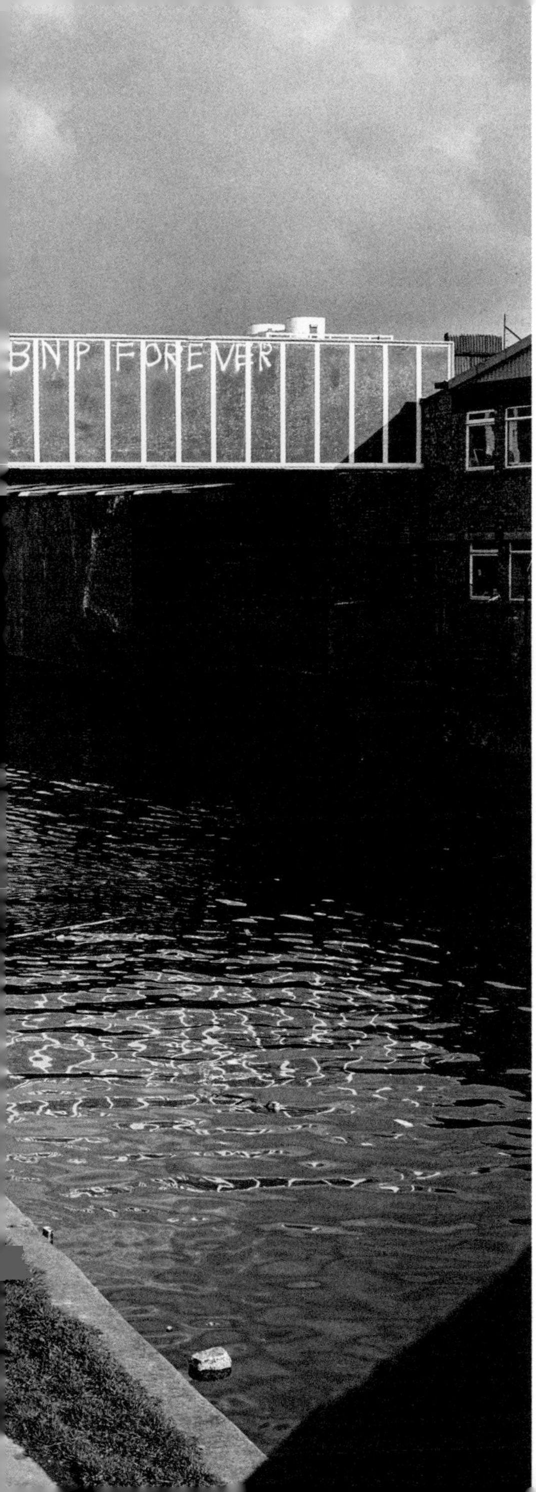
BNP FOREVER

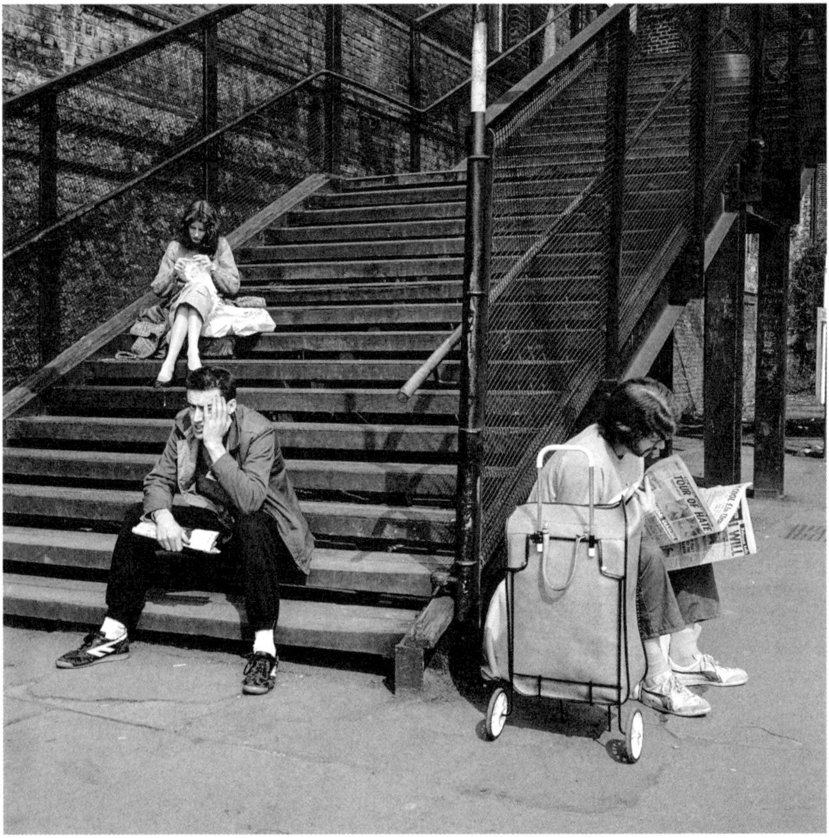
TOUR OF HATE

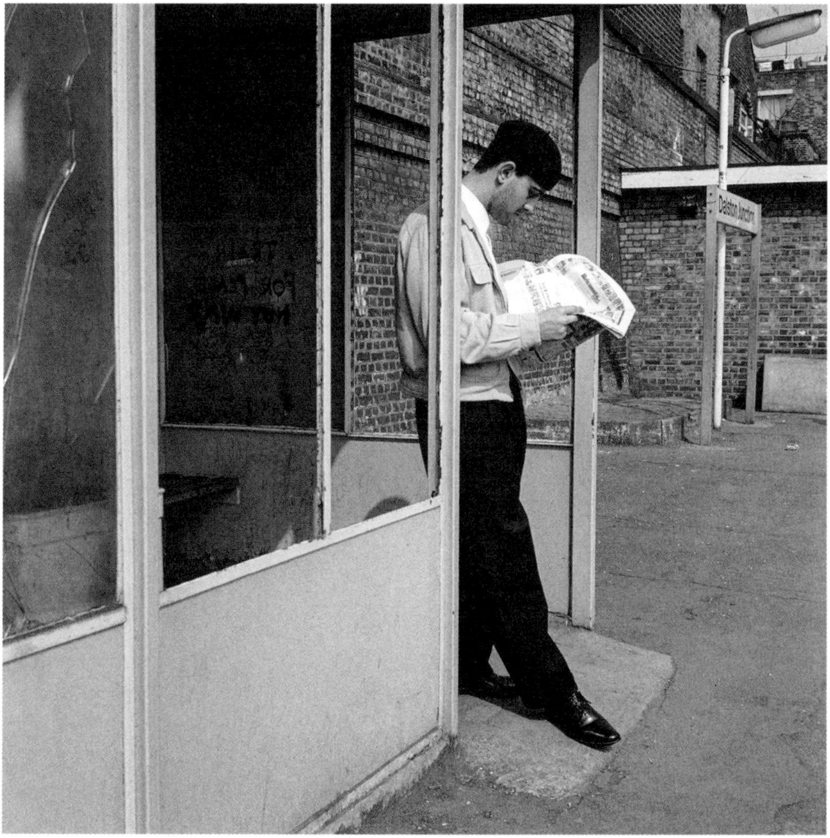
Dalston Junction

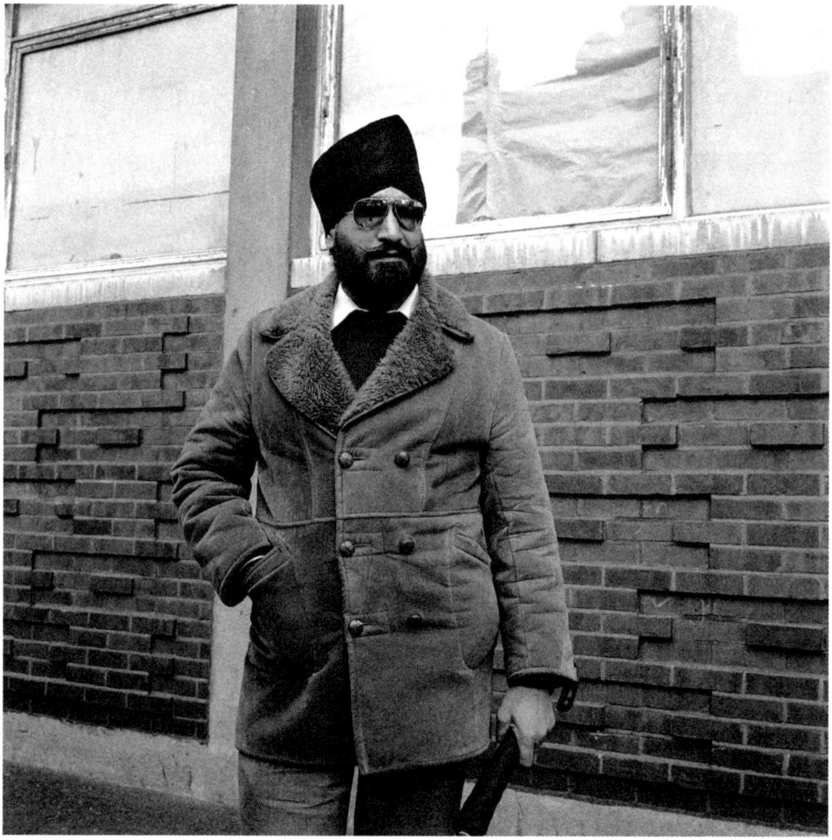

I used to go down Ridley Road Market
to catch a bus from Kingsland Road
to Old Street and then walk
through Smithfield meat market
to where I had a studio.

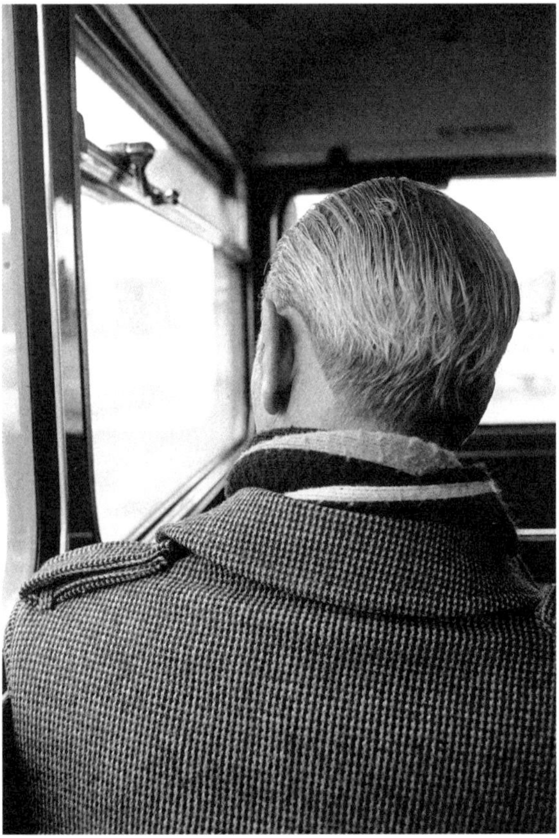

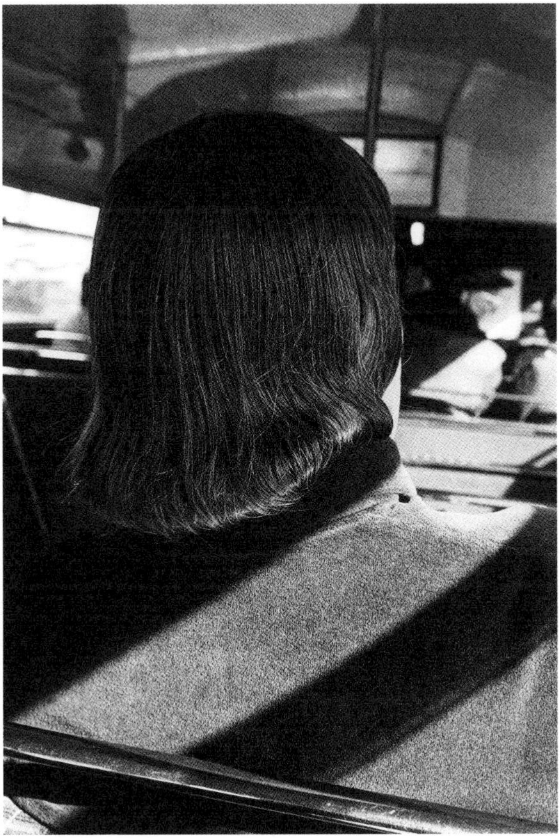

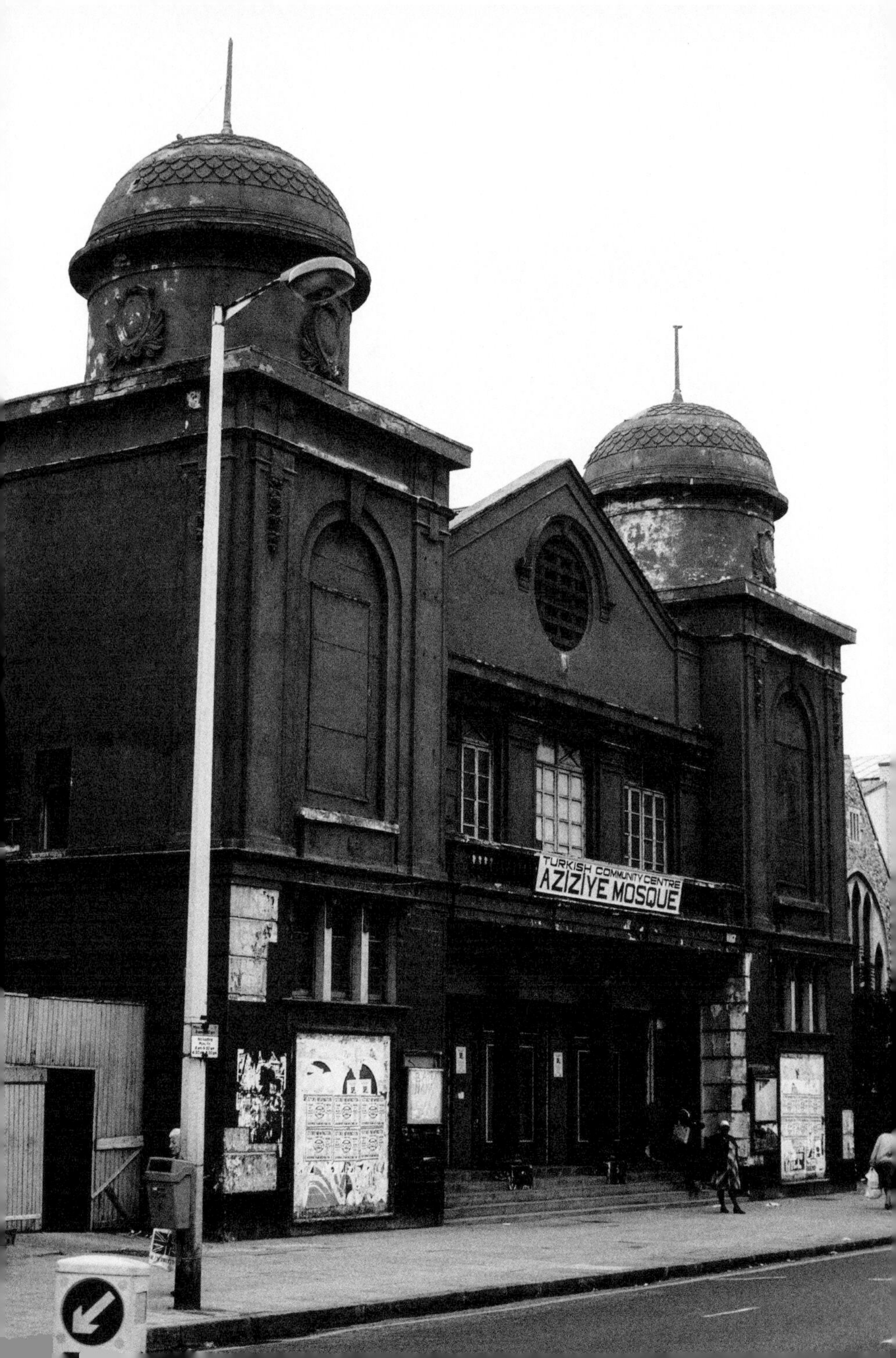
TURKISH COMMUNITY CENTRE
AZIZIYE MOSQUE

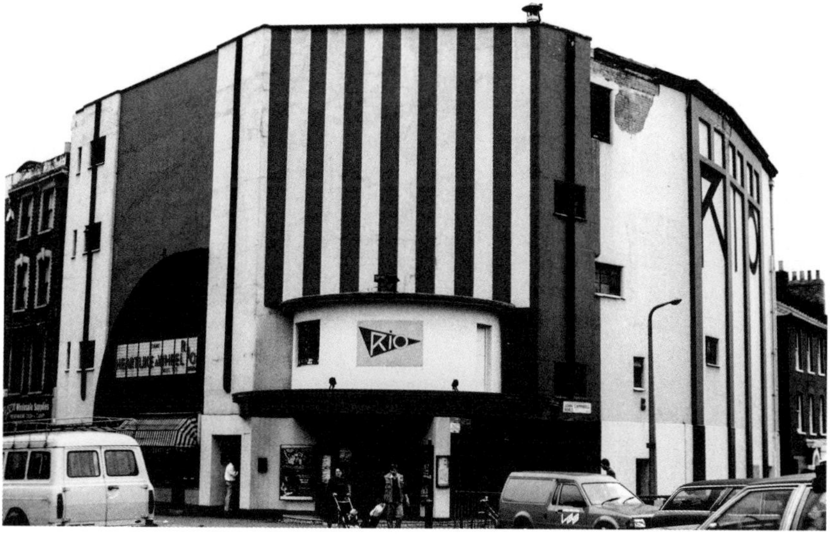
RIO
RIO

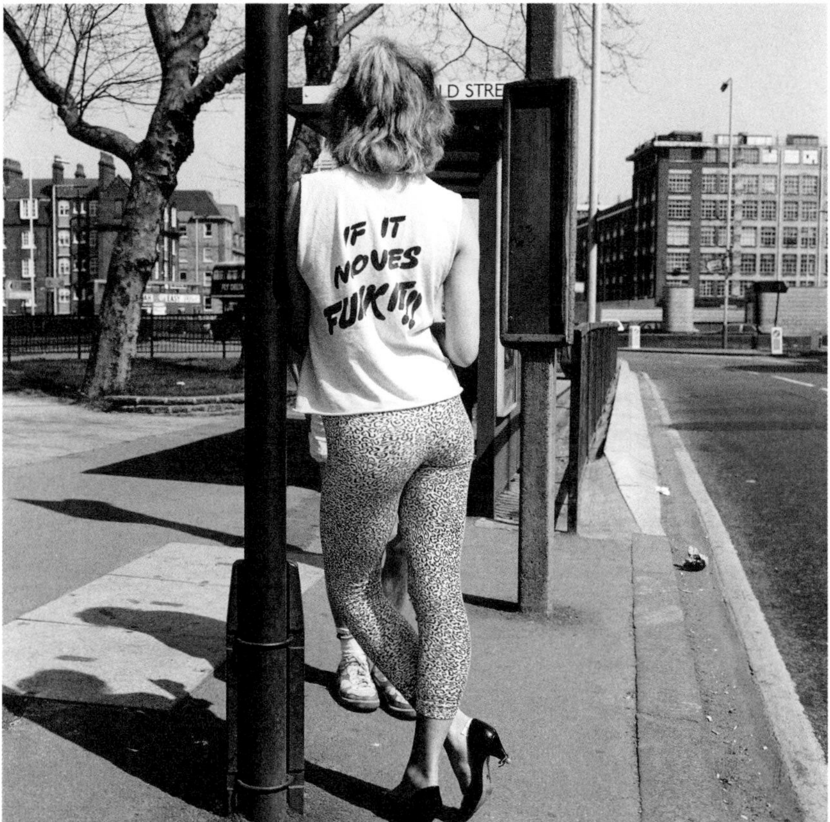
LD STRE
IF IT
MOVES
FUK IT!!

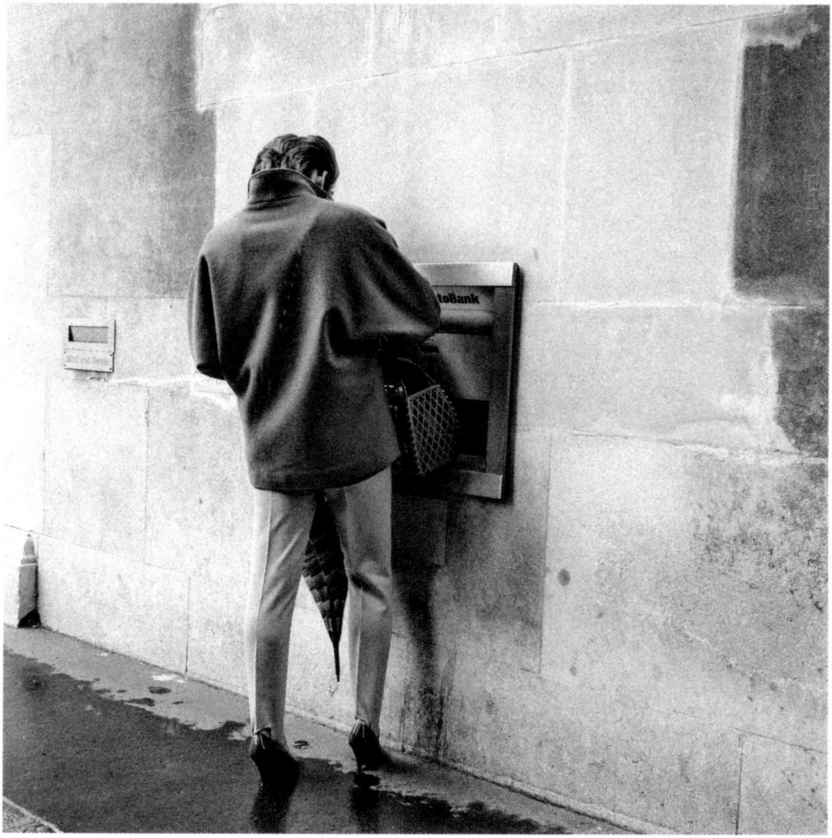

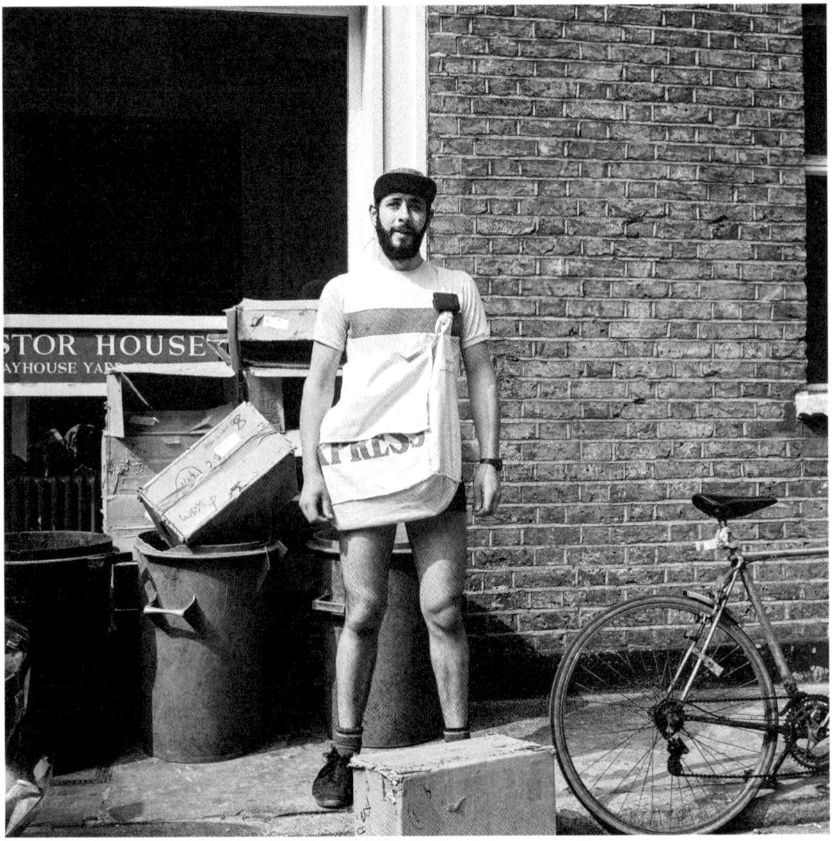
STOR HOUSE
AYHOUSE YAR
PRESS

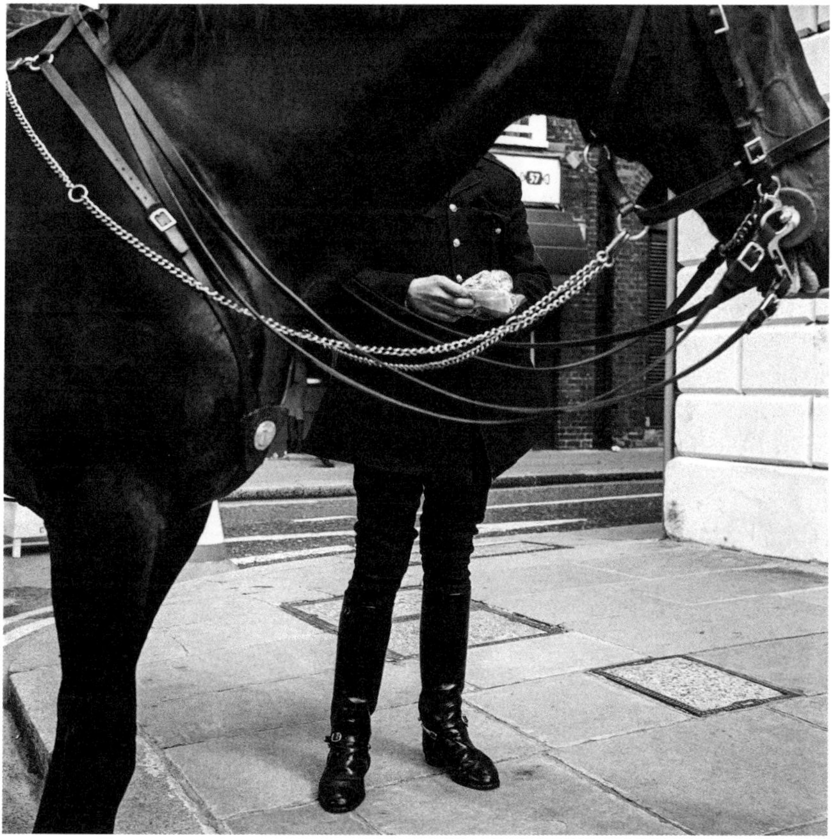
57

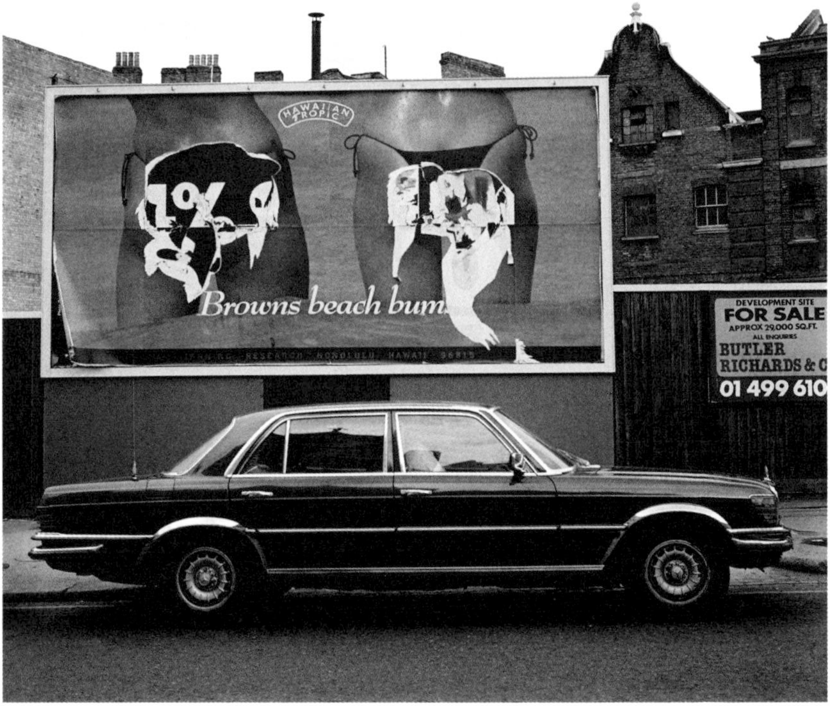
HAWAIIAN TROPIC
Browns beach bum
DEVELOPMENT SITE
FOR SALE
APPROX 29,000 SQ.FT.
ALL ENQUIRIES
BUTLER
RICHARDS & C
01 499 610

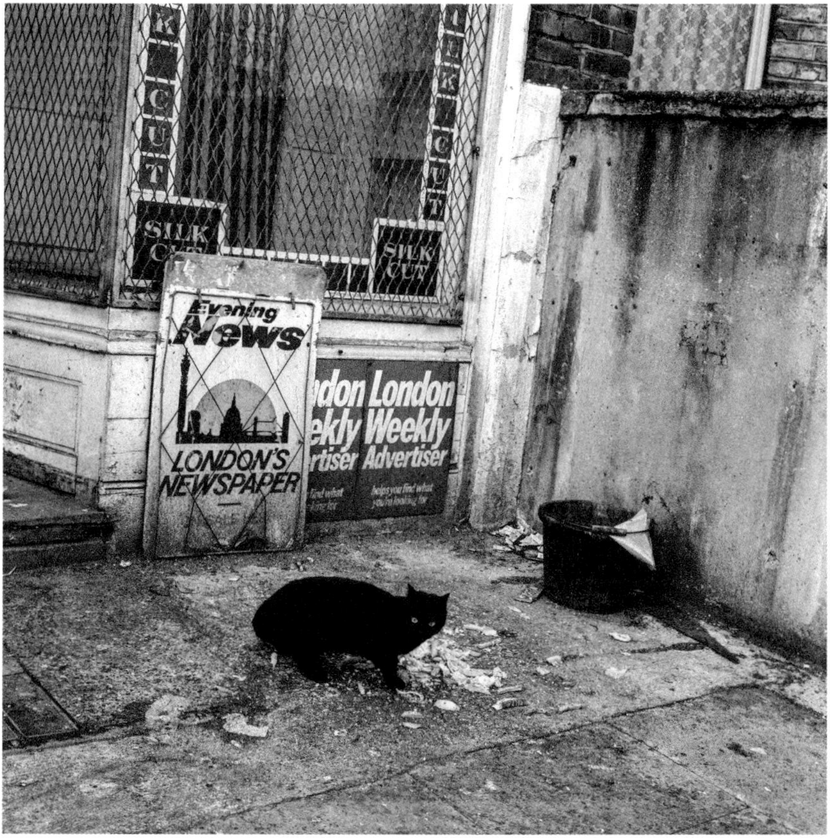
SILK CUT
SILK CUT
Evening News
LONDON'S NEWSPAPER
London Weekly Advertiser

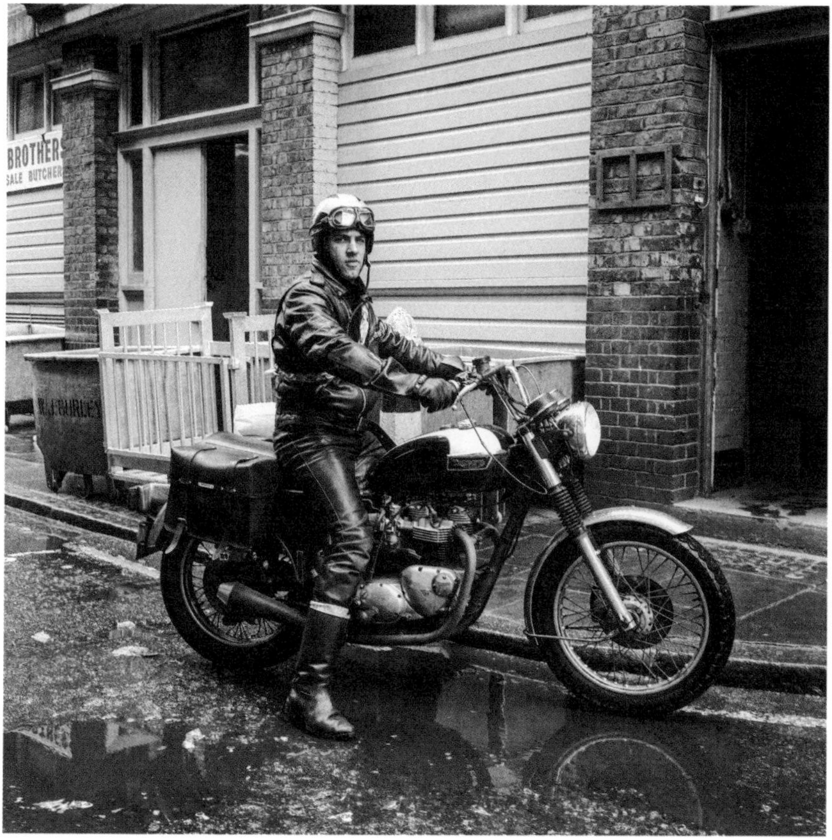

Danny, my cibachrome printer outside the studio just after the meat traders' daily hose-down.

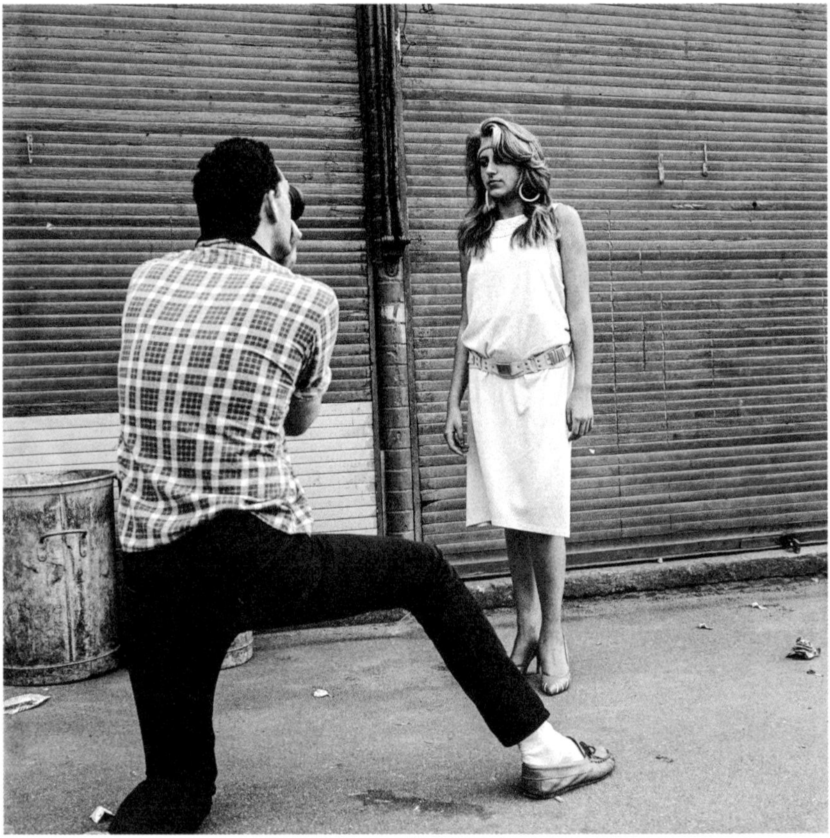

There was a porter at the meat market who wanted to be a fashion photographer, so I lent him a camera.

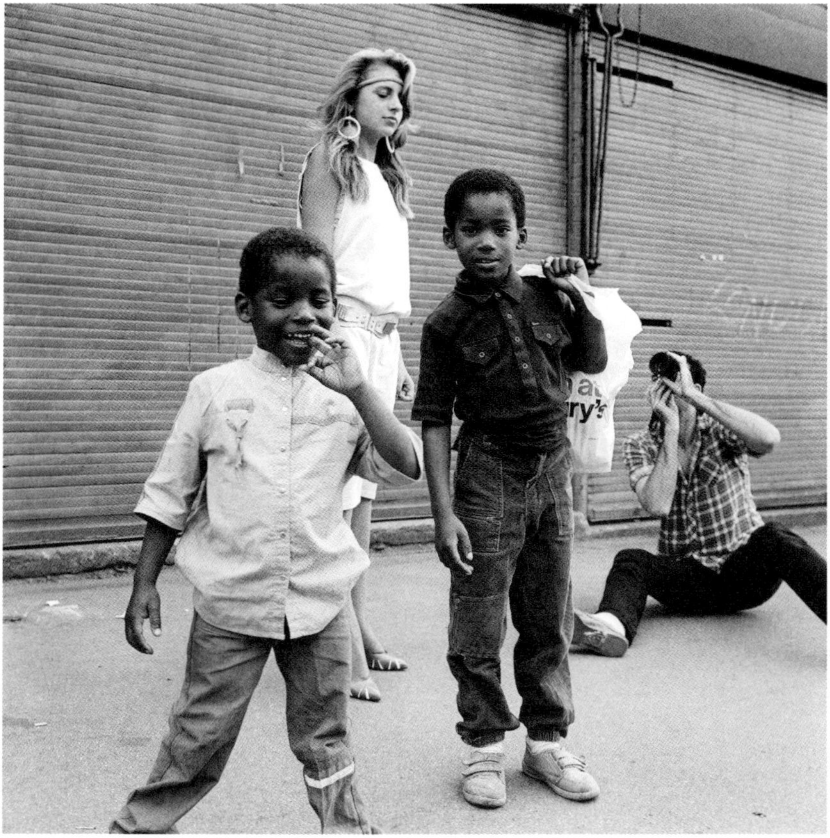

He found a Dalston girl
to model for him along Ridley Road
and two kids asked him;

"Are you David Bailey?"

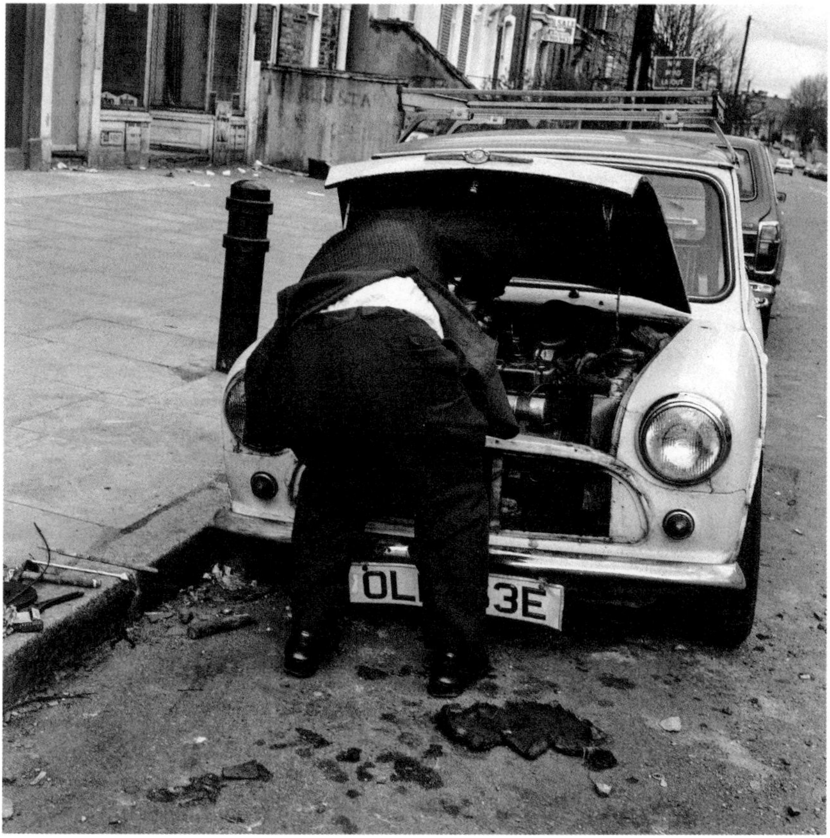

There he was, still fixing his Mini.
Maybe he was working for the KGB...

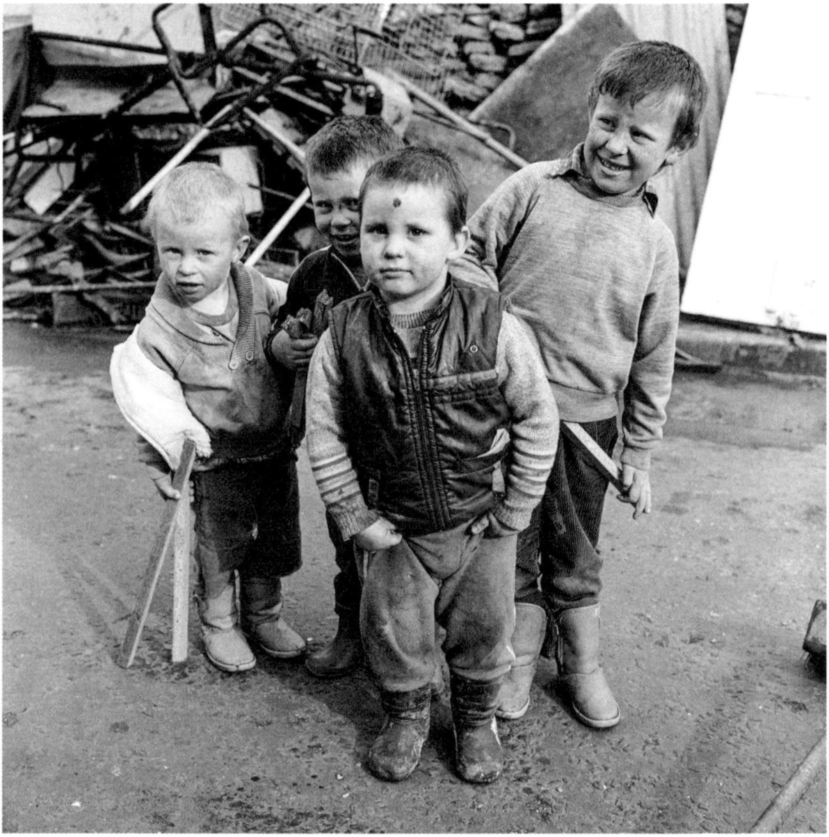

Sons

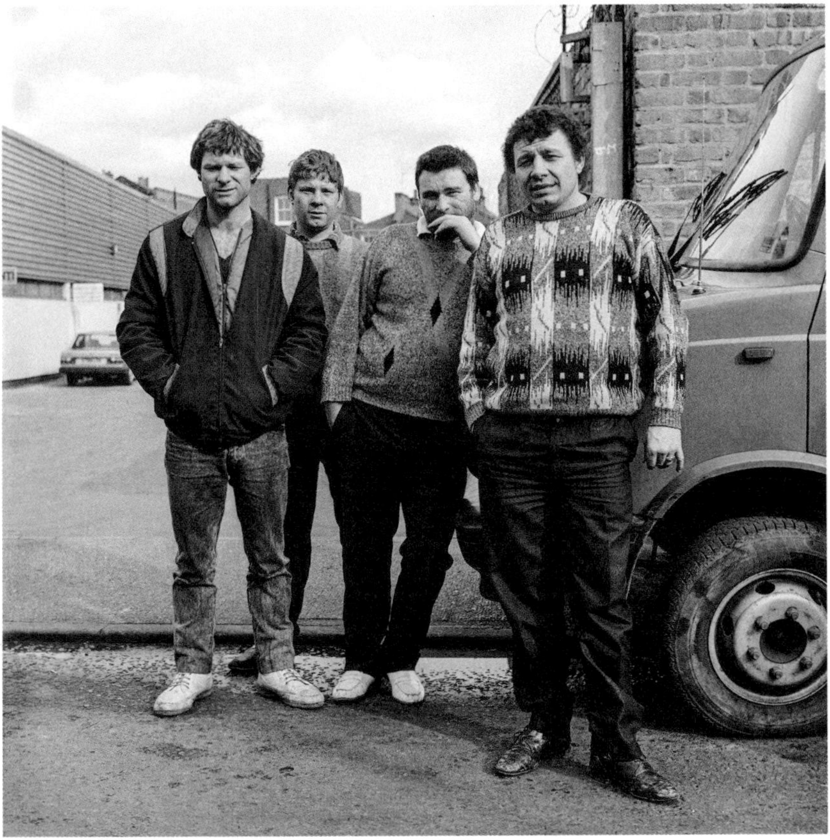

fathers

I left London for Sydney
in the wintry Spring of 1986.

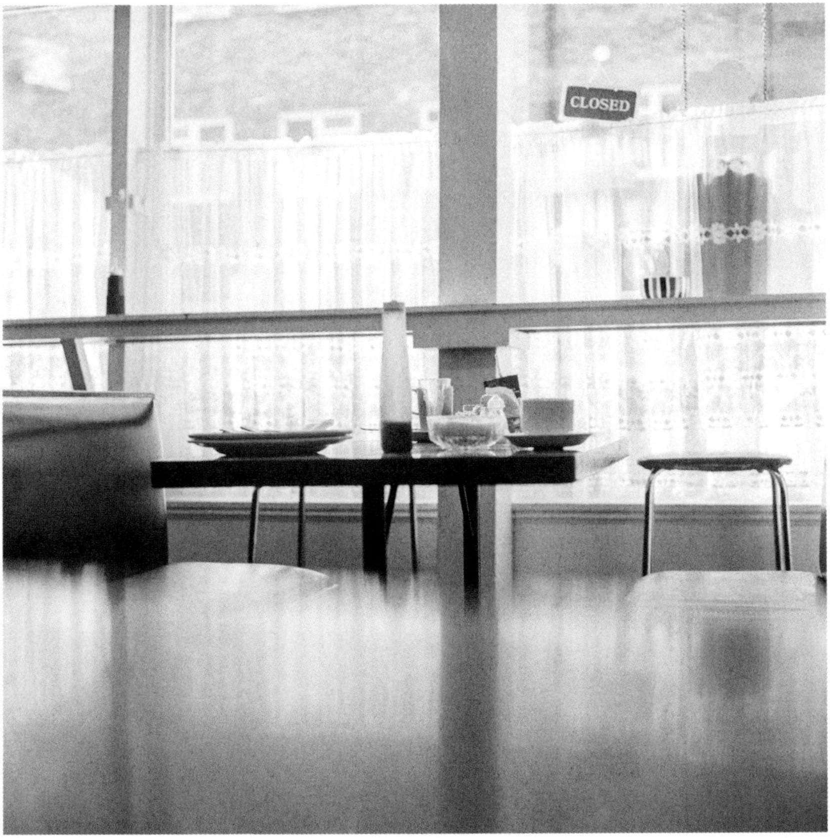

By then, my wife and I had gone our seperate ways

.. while my friend in California
had fallen in love and wanted
to sell his Dalston flat.

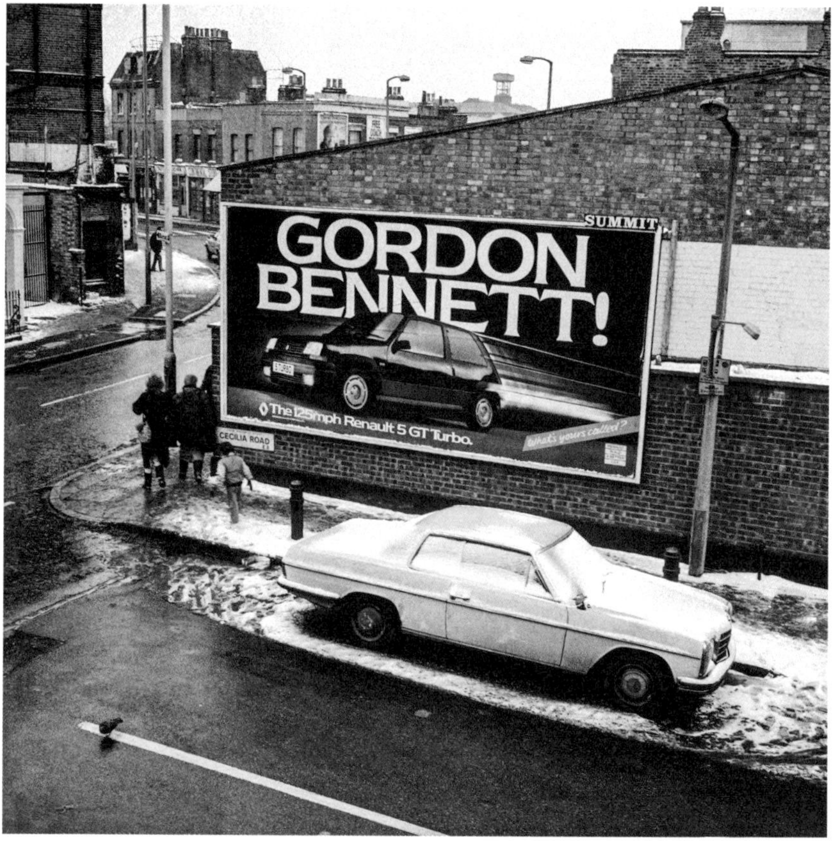
SUMMIT
GORDON BENNETT!
The 125mph Renault 5 GT Turbo.
what's yours called?
CECILIA ROAD

On the day I left for Heathrow,
I took a few final photos
from the kitchen window.

A couple of days later,
I was in bright light and blazing heat,
crossing Sydney Harbour on a ferry
with my old Rollei to hand.

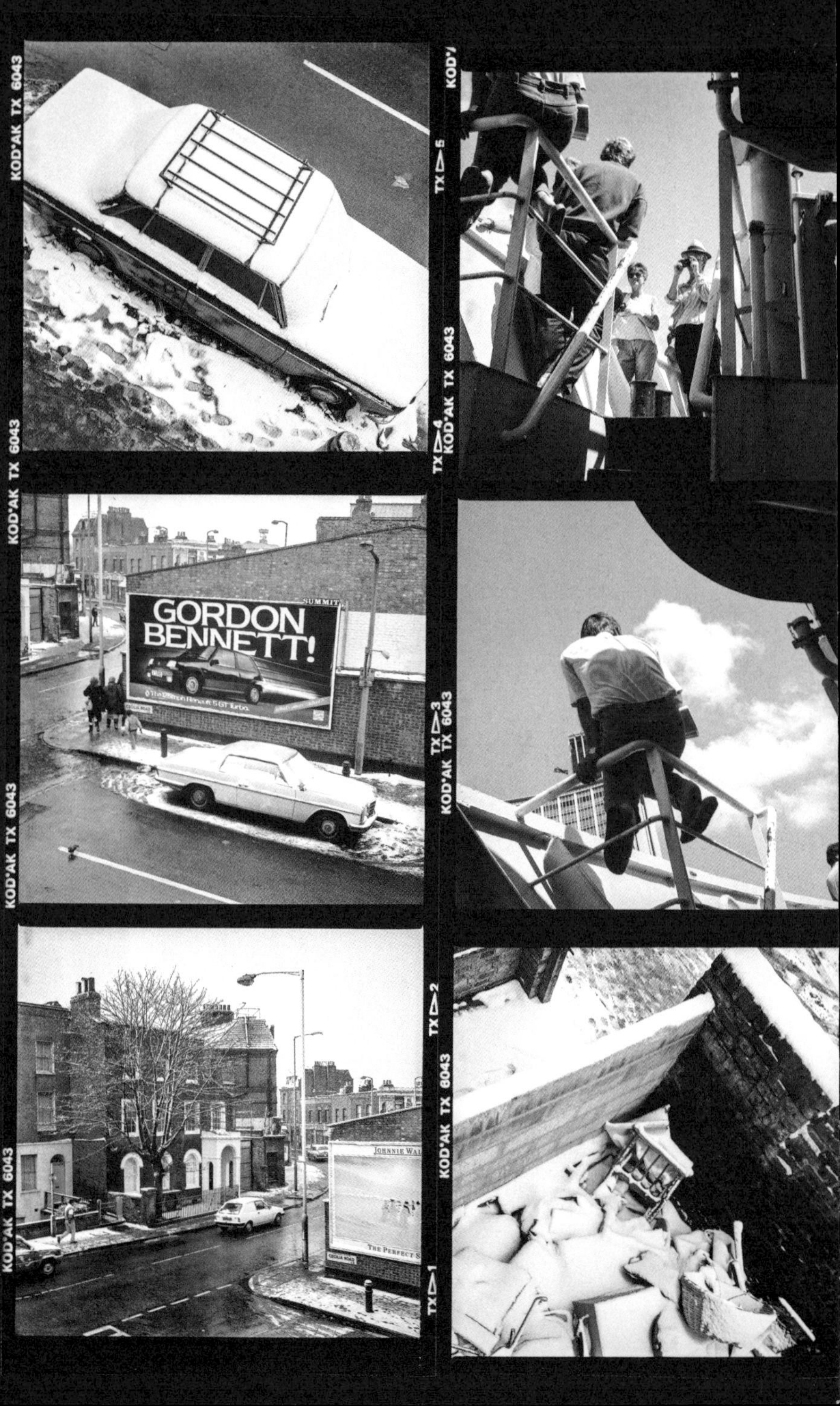
GORDON
BENNETT!
SUMMIT

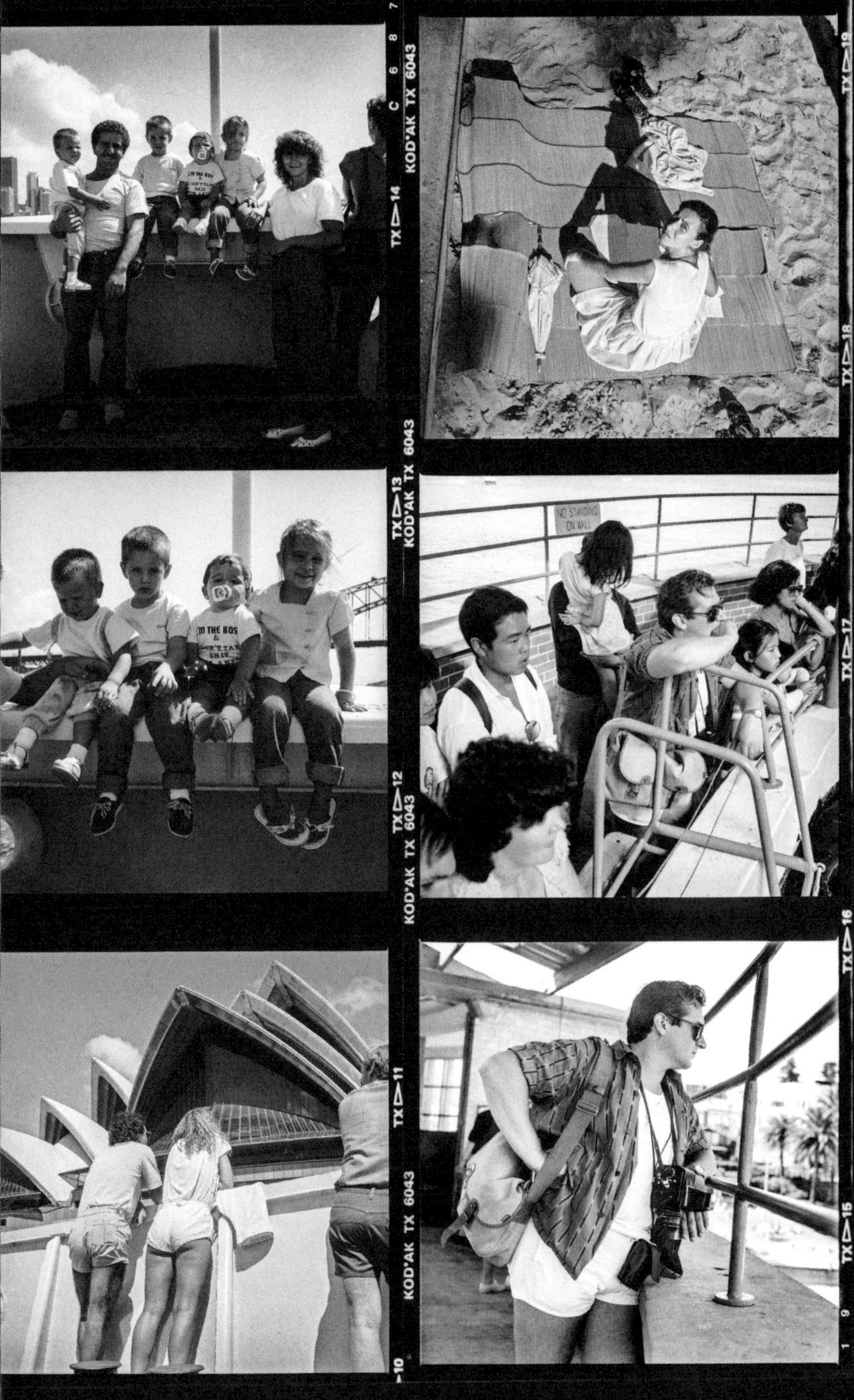
KOD'AK TX 6043
NO STANDING ON WALL
I'M THE BOSS

Photography is to me,
what Paris was to Ernest Hemingway
– a moveable feast –
that stays with you wherever you go.